# The
# Way
## of the
# Goddess

# The
# Way
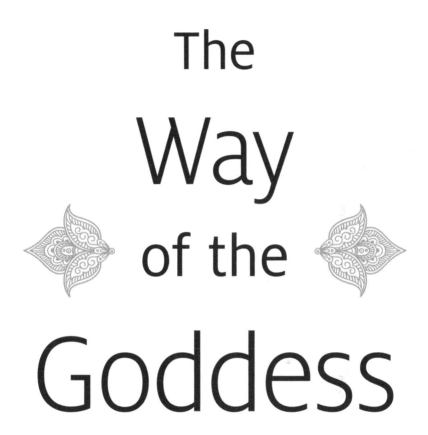
## of the
# Goddess

**Daily Rituals to Awaken Your Inner Warrior
and Discover Your True Self**

Ananta Ripa Ajmera

**with illustrations by Gaby Gohlar**

**A TarcherPerigee Book**

**tarcherperigee**

An imprint of Penguin Random House LLC
penguinrandomhouse.com

Most TarcherPerigee books are available at special quantity discounts for bulk
purchase for sales promotions, premiums, fundraising, and educational needs. Special
books or book excerpts also can be created to fit specific needs. For details, write:
SpecialMarkets@penguinrandomhouse.com.

Library of Congress Cataloging-in-Publication Data
Names: Ajmera, Ananta Ripa, author. | Gohlar, Gaby, illustrator.
Title: The way of the goddess: daily rituals to awaken your inner warrior and
discover your true self / Ananta Ripa Ajmera; with illustrations by Gaby Gohlar.
Description: [New York, New York]: TarcherPerigee, an imprint of
Penguin Random House LLC, [2022] | "A TarcherPerigee book."
Identifiers: LCCN 2022008274 (print) | LCCN 2022008275 (ebook) |
ISBN 9780593420706 (hardcover) | ISBN 9780593420713 (epub)
Subjects: LCSH: Self-realization—Religious aspects—Hinduism. |
Self-help techniques—Religious aspects—Hinduism. |
Hindu goddesses—India—Miscellanea. | Spiritual exercises.
Classification: LCC BL1238.34.A46 2022 (print) | LCC BL1238.34 (ebook) |
DDC 294.5/44—dc23/eng/20220611
LC record available at https://lccn.loc.gov/2022008274
LC ebook record available at https://lccn.loc.gov/2022008275

Printed in the United States of America
1st Printing

Book design by Shannon Nicole Plunkett

The greatest teachers are those who push
you to own your true power.

I dedicate this book to all the great
teachers in my life, who served as catalysts
for my awakening to the power of
Goddess Durga within me.

# Contents

Introduction ~ 1

*OM Sarva Mangala Mangalye Shive Sarvartha Sadhike*

*Sharanye Tryambake Gauri Narayani Namo'stute*

*I salute the Divine Mother, who brings total auspiciousness and who fulfills the desire for liberation.*

*Realization arises with Her blessing.*

*She is the world itself.*

*Only through the experiences of life can the soul be perfected.*

*Honor this gift, your life, bow to Mother Nature.*

DURGA SAPTASHATI, chapter 11

# Introduction

LONG BEFORE I UNDERSTOOD WHAT WE WERE CELEBRATING, NAVRATRI meant pomegranate seeds, potatoes, and puffed rice late at night after *garba* dancing (a traditional form of folk dancing from India) in a circle around the bright flame of a lamp in the center.

During the annual nine-night goddess festival that occurred every fall, the local Hindu community gathered at the high school basketball courts we converted into dance floors in Toledo, Ohio, where I grew up. Indian "aunties" (women I was not actually related to but called Auntie because that is what we call all women of our mothers' generation) pushed and pulled us children into the circle. I tried to say no–"We'll dance later, Auntie. Not right now, please!"–but it never worked. Garba dancing was a command performance, and the entire community, both men and women, came together to celebrate the divine feminine.

Though the food was delicious and the dancing magical, the truth was that I never really understood what the goddesses were all about. Some of the celebration was focused on a mother goddess, Durga, while other parts focused on individual goddesses who represented parts of Durga.

Some, like Saraswati, were pure and simple, while others were lavishly dressed and sat atop fearsome bulls or tigers. Several of the goddesses appeared soft, beautiful, and feminine, while others were downright intimidating, carrying swords, shields, maces, and other weapons. Kali was, by far, the fiercest and freakiest of all–she was armed and always depicted with her tongue sticking out, her foot atop a scary-looking demon. Bewildered or sometimes even frightened, I used to stare at these images during *aartis*, the worship rituals in which we would offer the flame of an earthen clay lamp to one or more deities. I knew I was supposed to feel something, but I mostly felt confused.

That confusion and frustration only grew over the years as I came to see the contrast between the reverence shown toward the goddesses during the festivals and the way girls and women were often treated in real life. My own childhood and adolescence had been marked by sexual and psychological trauma, eating disorders, and anxiety that left me adrift and constantly seeking an elusive inner peace that always seemed out of reach even once I left home and began my studies at New York University.

During my junior year, I traveled to India to research girls' education NGOs. On the last day of my trip, an Indian American volunteer named Heena took me on a tour of the Gandhi Ashram, where swarms of colorfully dressed children greeted us at every turn. When I pulled out a camera, they squealed with delight.

"Didi [elder sister], Didi, hi! Please take my photo!" they screamed. Laughing, I snapped as many pictures as I could, but as I looked through the viewfinder, I noticed one girl, about eight or nine years old, who hid and seemed dejected even as the other children sang and played.

When I asked Heena about her, she said somberly, "Her name is Lakshmi. She was raped last year. Her parents sent her here so that she would be safer and could get an education and have a better life, but even after six months, she is still withdrawn."

I instantly thought of Navratri and the colorful depictions of Lakshmi, the Hindu goddess of wealth. Traditional images show a strong, benevolent woman sitting on a lion, bedecked in jewels with coins falling from her hands. The fact that this little girl had been abused and yet was named after the most widely worshipped Hindu goddess struck me like a lightning bolt. Why could we not connect the divine feminine that we worshipped during Navratri to the divine feminine inside this little girl, inside all little girls and women? Was there a way to not just worship the idea of the divine feminine but also to find it in ourselves and to carry that strength with us into the modern world?

When I returned to NYU, I couldn't stop thinking about Lakshmi. One night, I walked into a bookstore where I discovered a deck of goddess guidance oracle cards. Sure enough, in the deck was a beautiful image of the goddess Lakshmi, wearing a yellow sari and a crown, a bright sun rising behind her, elephants in the background, and lotus flowers in both of her hands. The card's message was "Bright Future." Inside the accompanying booklet was a note about Lakshmi that shared how "[she] is a beautiful and benevolent Hindu goddess who brings abundance to those who call upon her. Lakshmi works with Ganesh, the elephant-headed deity who's known as the 'remover of obstacles.' Together, they're an unstoppable team that works to help you release fear and accept abundance."

Looking at the card that night and in the months and years that came after, I wondered what a "Bright Future" really meant. Instead of pursuing a career in finance as my parents had expected, I graduated from college in 2008 and then studied Yoga and Ayurveda in India before moving to San Francisco in 2009 to teach youth in detention centers. I knew that finding the way forward on this unconventional path would pose challenges, but I forged ahead, following my heart and delving into ancient texts and traditions during my studies. As I learned more about what the goddesses represented, I came to understand that Navratri, the goddesses, and the divine feminine weren't something to be celebrated just once a year. Instead, they could be the foundation for daily practices that would eventually fill my days with a strength and confidence I had never before known.

## About This Book

The journey of Navratri is ultimately one of moving from darkness to light, from being disconnected from your true Self to knowing yourself, trusting yourself, and connecting the divinity inside you to the way in which you think, feel, and behave every day. This union with the higher Self is the heart of the nine-day cycle, and this book is both the story of how I discovered my higher Self through this practice and a practical, actionable guide for how you can too.

The wisdom in the pages that follow is rooted in the Vedic spiritual tradition, the universal spirituality of India based in the Vedas, which are the world's oldest sacred texts that serve as the fountainhead for four world religions from India–Hinduism, Buddhism, Sikhism, and Jainism. But the practice itself is also firmly grounded in my own hard-won experience. My move to California in 2009 was the first step on a decade-long journey I took to heal from childhood trauma and to connect with my higher Self.

Early on in my studies, I discovered that the goddesses are not only nurturers but also warriors. Durga, who is traditionally known as the mother of the universe, is said to possess all the powers of the gods and is frequently depicted riding a lion or tiger and carrying a multitude of weapons. The ancient stories clearly identify her as female to help us humans understand the genderless divine in a way we can more easily relate to, but Durga's transformative power is not only available to women or those who identify as women. I believe that Durga is available and accessible to all modern seekers, no matter their gender identity, because she is emblematic of the power each and every one of us has to give birth to the most authentic version of ourselves (which the light of the lamp of the garba dance represents).

Though I do use she/her/hers pronouns and terms like *goddess*, *mother*, and *woman*, all are welcome on this journey. The Navratri practice is far more expansive and inclusive than the tradition suggests, and I believe that even though many of the ancient stories depict heteronormative love to make a point, these tales are more allegorical than literal. Every offering, every example, every practice in this book is available to anyone who wants to walk the path of the Navratri practice in an effort to know themselves.

Indian mythology tells the story of how Durga battled various demons during the course of nine nights, culminating with her victory over the most terrible demon on the tenth night. Each night of the traditional Navratri festival, a different aspect of Durga's infinite strength emerges through the goddesses who represent various aspects of the spiritual journey we must all undertake in order to attain abiding health and to realize the truth of who we really are.

The demons Durga and her goddess avatars fight are deeply symbolic of the demons we must confront within ourselves: the demons of excessive anger, fear, lust, jealousy, insecurity, hatred, greed, delusions, and depression. Only by waging these inner battles and defeating these demons will we recognize our true Self as an unchanging, eternal soul–not merely a decaying body and constantly changing mind.

Though the Vedic spiritual tradition encompasses a wealth of rituals to facilitate these struggles for spiritual development and wellness, the more I learned, the more I wanted something that went beyond the tradition, something personalized to me and my modern life. Through experimentation and intuition, I expanded the annual nine-day festival into a daily Navratri practice, during which I remember a particular goddess each morning and strive during the day to embody the virtue she represents, in both small and big ways.

Throughout the year, I follow this nine-day cycle as if it were always Navratri, which to me has come to mean that every day is an opportunity to celebrate the divine feminine in myself and others. While that sometimes means being soft and more traditionally feminine, I have found that I can and must also be a spiritual warrior in order to emulate and celebrate Durga. Cultivating both strength and softness as part of this practice has changed my life.

> Every day is an opportunity to celebrate the divine feminine in myself and others.

Through my work with individuals and groups, I've seen that this process can change other lives as well. My students tell me it is flexible and adaptable enough for them to bring the goddesses into their own lives in ways that are as authentic and meaningful for them as my practice is to me, even for individuals who know nothing at first about Navratri, goddesses, Yoga, or Ayurveda. My aim in this book is for these rituals to be as accessible and transformative today as they have been for thousands of years.

In each chapter, you'll meet one goddess, hear her story, and discover powers you can identify and cultivate within yourself. You'll also learn more about the four goals of life, which, according to the Vedas, are purpose, abundance, pleasure, and spiritual liberation, and the ways the goddesses can help you achieve these goals for yourself.

Each of the nine chapters begins with an introduction to a goddess and the power she represents. Then, you'll have the opportunity to take

# THE FOUR GOALS OF LIFE

The Vedic spiritual tradition has given us four universal goals of life that this book's practices encompass.

PURPOSE. This is about living your life according to your deepest values and giving back to others in a way that feels personally meaningful. We need values as an anchor to navigate the many uncertainties of modern life with inner strength, clarity, and a sense of reassurance, no matter what happens in the world around us.

ABUNDANCE. This goal is about gaining material and emotional security through your work and relationships. Abundance is necessary to live in the modern world and is what gives you the ability to not only work to earn a living but also to give back to others and be able to pursue spiritual knowledge.

PLEASURE. It may seem surprising, but pleasure is just as valid a life goal as the other three, as the Vedic spiritual tradition does not see anything wrong with enjoyment. Ancient Vedic wisdom has given us great guidance in terms of applying our code of purposeful values to the realm of enjoyment, ensuring we don't get enslaved by cravings and obsessions for more pleasure.

SPIRITUAL LIBERATION. Knowing who you truly are as a spiritual being is deemed the highest and ultimate goal of human life in the Vedic spiritual tradition. It is an important quest in our modern lives, which are full of so many distractions that lead us to forget our true spiritual power, the forgetting of which leads to so much psychological and even physiological suffering.

inventory of your current relationship to that power as it manifests in your own life. I encourage you to use a journal to answer these questions so that you have a record of your process of transformation. Next, I discuss how to cultivate that power in your own life and why it's important. And finally, I discuss the path forward and recommend nine practices that will bolster your connection to that power and to the associated chakra. For deeper exploration, my organization, The Ancient Way, has a Spiritual Warrior Certificate Program you are welcome to join.

The practices in each chapter are also designed to balance one of your *chakras* (a Sanskrit word meaning "wheel"). A chakra is a spinning vortex of energy that is said to regulate not only physiological but also psychological functions. The chakras are said to represent the different layers of your mind that you can bring into balance for overall well-being at all levels: body, mind, and intellect. There is a different goddess and power that unfolds within you when you work to balance each chakra.

I recommend you read the chapters in order, as there is a systematic progression from one to the next. However, the chapters are also cyclical in nature, and with time and experience, you can return to them in whatever order you prefer, whether you are a beginner or have been studying spirituality for many years.

You will find that the stories I tell about my own experiences are generally but not perfectly chronological. As with any significant change, my progress was not linear. While some practices and shifts were easier for me to adopt, others took years of practice and contemplation to implement. My own story is cyclical, as yours will likely be, and in order to portray the reality of my own journey, I do occasionally move back and forth in time even though the stories roughly appear in the order in which they occurred.

As you read through the book the first time, try one practice after finishing each chapter to experience what it's like to do something that balances each of your chakras in order. Don't overthink it–experience is the

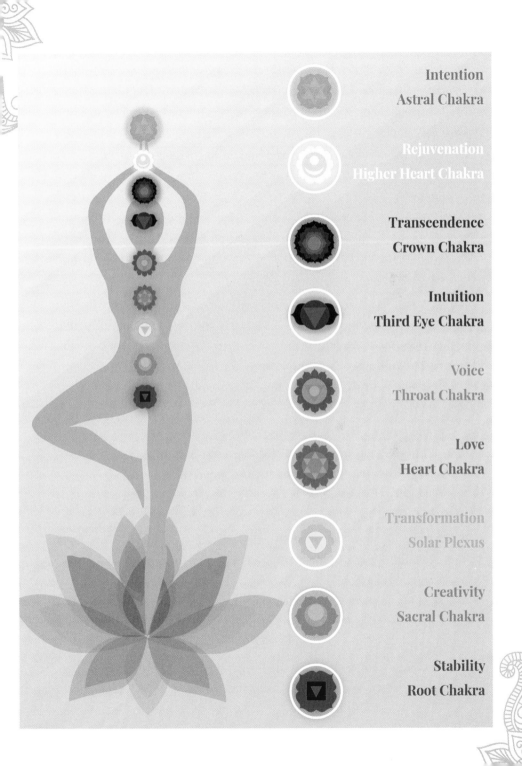

Intention
Astral Chakra

Rejuvenation
Higher Heart Chakra

**Transcendence**
**Crown Chakra**

**Intuition**
**Third Eye Chakra**

Voice
Throat Chakra

Love
Heart Chakra

Transformation
Solar Plexus

Creativity
Sacral Chakra

**Stability**
**Root Chakra**

best teacher, so choose the practice that seems most appealing to you in the moment. After you finish trying out nine different practices for each of the nine chakras at your own pace, you will be encouraged to celebrate your personal victories in the conclusion. Each nine-day cycle is followed by a Sabbath, a day of reflection and celebration of the light over darkness in our lives. It is also an opportunity to recommit yourself to a new cycle of practice.

For example, say you struggle with anxiety, and you've picked up this book looking for ways to alleviate that feeling. On the first day of the Navratri practice, you can start by rooting your feet into Mother Earth to cultivate the power of stability.

Then you can work on channeling your anxious energy with the buzzing-bee breathing exercise to balance your second chakra, which fosters the power of creativity.

Then as the third step, which is about balancing your solar plexus with the power of transformation, you can light a lamp with the intention of burning away your anxiety.

On the fourth step, which focuses on the power of love, you can focus on listening to soothing music you love to help calm your mind.

On the fifth step, which is about the power of your voice, you can practice writing a letter to your anxiety, recognizing how it has helped you survive and what it is preventing you from doing now.

Then as you approach the sixth step, which cultivates the power of your intuition, you can focus on spending less time with people who make you feel anxious.

On the seventh step, which is about the power of transcendence, you can focus on repeating the mantra "I am a soul" to strengthen your spiritual power and your true identity as a soul to transcend your anxiety.

The eighth step, which is about new beginnings via the power of rejuvenation, is when you can dance away your anxiety.

On the ninth step, which is about the power of intention, you can write down your intention to further your spiritual growth and thereby reduce your anxiety.

Then on the tenth step, which is about celebrating overcoming the obstacles in your life, you can celebrate your progress toward releasing your anxiety. And then you can begin a new cycle, with all of the same, completely different, or a mixture of tried and new practices.

It is best to make changes in your lifestyle gradually, to ensure that you are able to sustain new habits and enjoy the deepest possible benefits over time. You can return to this book again and again as a reference for accessing the divinity that lives within you.

As you move forward, don't worry if you can't do your practice(s) every single day. Simply set an intention to be consistent in what you have chosen and begin again as soon as you can. This will help prevent getting into an "all or nothing" mode, and you will still benefit from living the process of transformation and from expanding your sense of what's possible for you, one day and one step at a time. Even though I myself do one practice each day, it took me more than a decade to arrive at this place. Be patient and loving with yourself, and you will find a rhythm that works for you, whether you create a nine-day cycle like I have or choose a nine-week or even a nine-month cycle after experimenting with the ideas in this book.

I invite and encourage you to develop a practice that feels right and doable for you, one that you can own. I share my experiences and stories of applying the different practices over the course of eleven years as a guide for you to also live in a healthier, more empowered, and freer way.

## About Me

I first experienced Navratri as a catalyst for spiritual transformation while studying Yoga, Ayurveda, and Vedanta for nine years in a spiritual lineage stemming back to ancient India. Today, I lead my own organization where I share the teachings I received using my own words and recipes and with nothing but immense gratitude for all that I have learned from others. The word *guru* means "remover of darkness," and for many years, I saw myself primarily as a student even as I began teaching and leading others. But writing this book has served as a powerful catalyst for my own transformation and has culminated in my awakening to my own inner guru: the sole purpose of a spiritual quest.

I continue to learn and study, because the more we learn of spirituality, the more we realize how much we do not know. Continuously pursuing my own studies also empowers me to lead and teach with wisdom, humility, and integrity. When I moved to New York in 2019, I was blessed to meet Swami Parthasarathy, a philosopher-saint considered to be one of the leading exponents of Vedanta philosophy. I started studying in the three-year recorded online program of his organization, Vedanta World.

It is important for readers new to Ayurveda, Yoga, and Vedanta to know that everything I learned from my first teacher and from Swami Parthasarathy is based on oral tradition, passed down from teacher to student in unbroken lineages since time immemorial. The ultimate authority of these teachings is contained in sacred source texts that were divinely revealed to sages in the depths of their meditations in ancient India.

Though I have tremendous love and respect for the knowledge contained in all the texts, for me, the most important aspect of my studies has been embodying and practicing what I've learned. It is through the applied practice of Ayurveda, integrated with Yoga and Vedanta, that I have been able to heal from ancestral trauma, relationship abuse of all kinds, and eating disorders, by remembering the power of the goddess within me, as my own soul's power.

Each chapter of this book walks you through the process of how I embodied one of the incredible verses of the Bhagavad Gita, a well-known Vedic spiritual text. The stories in the Gita take place on a battlefield, which is symbolic of the battles we fight in our daily lives. In this epic spiritual text, Lord Krishna guides his warrior student Arjuna to battle his corrupt cousins for the sake of his kingdom, which his cousins wrongfully seized from him. Though Arjuna is a renowned warrior, he is gripped by fear and attachment at the prospect of going to war because he doesn't want to hurt his family members and archery teacher on the other side. To fight–and win–this battle, Lord Krishna guides Arjuna step-by-step to first and foremost win the war within himself by conquering his desires and reconnecting with his true Self. Like Arjuna, I too had to overcome my fears and attachments toward my family members and others in order to discover my true Self.

In the spiritual teachings of Vedanta, there is a term, *samsara*, that means the endless ocean of our self-created illusions and projections onto reality, which create our suffering. Before I began my studies, I was drowning in samsara, and this book tells the story of how I went to the very depths of the ocean to uncover the pearl of my true Self at the bottom. Just as each chapter teaches about one aspect of Durga, each chapter also chronicles my own personal journey from darkness to light, to give you inspiration and hope that, by applying the same ancient wisdom to your modern life, you too can successfully navigate the ocean of samsara, whatever that means for you, and begin to discover your true Self.

I developed this book to also support you in planting beautiful seeds of new practices that you can integrate in your own life, to grow your own gorgeous garden of well-being, from the inside out. The practices are cyclical, infinite, and designed to meet you where you are.

I am so honored and delighted to extend my hands to you to join a community wellness movement and be part of a sacred, endless circular dance of life. May you light a bright lamp of hope in your heart that will ignite your spiritual awareness and resolve so that you can ultimately realize your divine potential and activate from within yourself your own radiant soul power.

# Chapter 1

# The Power of Practice

*The Self cannot be cut, nor burnt, nor wetted, nor dried.*
*The Self is eternal, all-pervading, stable, immovable and ancient.*

—BHAGAVAD GITA, chapter 2, verse 24

## Cultivating Stability

Stability means many things to many people, but on the spiritual path, it is the ability to remain focused on your objective no matter the obstacles that arise. Stability is rooted in the concept of *shraddha*, a Sanskrit term that represents the capacity of the intellect to reflect upon teachings, understand them, and make them your own. Shraddha is the ability to pursue knowledge until you become one with it, until the information brings about a transformation in your life, and mere knowledge metamorphoses into your living, embodied wisdom. In the Navratri practice, stability is the foundation for your entire journey. That's why we begin with getting grounded; your feet need to be planted in the ground, literally and metaphorically, to allow you to climb higher toward the ultimate goal of spiritual enlightenment.

Having the power of stability means being able to say yes to people, practices, and situations that support you on your quest for spiritual growth and saying no to what no longer serves you. But cultivating stability is not something that happens just once before you move ahead to something else. Instead, it's a first step you will take again and again as you navigate life's inevitable ups and downs. That's why getting grounded is the first step on the nine-step journey of Navratri practice; it is what enables you to commit yourself today (and again in the future) to living a life filled with purpose, abundance, pleasure, and liberation.

When I began to create this practice, I found myself thinking of the god and goddess look-alike contests that were part of my childhood experience of Navratri. One year my mother and her friend dressed me as Radha, the goddess consort of Lord Krishna who represents the power of devotion. They wrapped me in a gold-and-blue sari that exposed my stomach and attached to the bun in my hair. I was mortified to walk on-stage in this bizarre getup. And I was even more horrified when I was announced as the winner since then I had to pose for a photo with the winner of the Krishna look-alike competition.

Starting my nine years of lineage-based spiritual study was the beginning of my attempts to create stability in my own life. As I embarked on what would turn out to be a decade-long journey to true wellness, I looked back on those contests with a strange mix of longing and bemusement. On the outside, I had so closely resembled a goddess that I had won a prize, but on the inside, I felt nothing of Radha's divine nature. I was twenty-five years old and was in my first year of study. I knew that to others I appeared accomplished and calm, but inside I felt disconnected from my true Self, afraid to know her and to confront the pain that I carried with me from a difficult childhood. As I learned and studied more during those first months, I asked myself, "What if being like a goddess has nothing to do with appearance and everything to do with remaking myself from the inside out? What if, instead of searching outside of myself, I went inside to find my power and to find the goddess within?"

That for me was the start of a new life, and I began with Goddess Shailputri, who we celebrate on the first night of Navratri. She lives in your first chakra and helps you get grounded when you start balancing it, as I eventually did, with lifestyle practices that provide refuge amidst the many changes of life.

## Knowing SHAILPUTRI

Shailputri was a royal princess, and her father, Prajapati, was the king of all of humanity. He invited his subjects from far and wide to join him for festivals and celebrations and, most important, to serve him during these sacred occasions.

One day, Shailputri returned to visit her parents from her home in the Himalayas where she lived with her husband, Lord Shiva, the god of transformation. When she arrived, her father was organizing a great *yajna*, a huge fire ceremony into which all manner of material things were to be offered, including fruit, flowers, clothing, and money. The idea was that whatever the people let go of would return to them many times over.

Everyone in the world was invited, except for Lord Shiva. King Prajapati was embarrassed that his son-in-law wore leopard skin, had long hair, draped a serpent around his neck, and smeared his face with ashes. Prajapati could see only that Lord Shiva was different; he did not recognize that Lord Shiva was the embodiment of spirituality. He did not understand that the serpent Shiva wore around his neck symbolized how he had conquered his ego and was the master of his mind. He did not understand that Lord Shiva carried the entire holy Ganges River in his long hair, nor did he know of the great penance and spiritual discipline that Lord Shiva had performed, along with countless lifetimes of contemplation and meditation.

Prajapati's arrogance and ignorance outraged his daughter, and she stood up to her father. "Why have you not invited my husband? You've

made a great fire so you'll go to heaven, have good karma, and gain more material blessings, but there is nothing spiritual about this!"

Shailputri moved toward the fire to immolate herself in protest of her father's hypocrisy, but she did not actually need to step into the flames. She just said om and was consumed by the all-powerful inner fire of her desire for a new life, one in which she could live with a true sense of devotion and spirituality. She was then reborn as the daughter of the Himalayas and continued her spiritual journey unencumbered by the attachments to material things that had held her back as the daughter of the king.

Our desire for genuine transformation in the modern world is no less intense than Shailputri's and connects us through the millennia to her and to her story. Certainly, the idea of starting again without the parts of our lives that hold us back is enormously appealing. And yet we struggle to begin the process of transformation because to succeed in this endeavor, we must let go of aspects of our lives that are no longer working for us. It feels dramatic—and it is—but we must burn away our old ways to reclaim ourselves and to welcome a more spiritual way of living.

That's where stability comes in. Strip away the external markers of who we are—job, clothes, partners, etc.—and we are left with our core essence. When we connect with that core, we can finally, after years of focusing on the external, find peace by knowing the stability within. Shailputri is the perfect embodiment of this quality, which stems from a firm resolve and willingness to forgo ease in pursuit of a spiritual quest. The way forward may not be easy, but with time, consistency, and determination, being connected to and nurturing the stability within you will create a new and deeper kind of comfort. Such is the power of Shailputri.

In addition to representing stability, Goddess Shailputri is also a divine embodiment of our perfect Mother Earth. I refer to Mother Earth, Mother Nature, and Shailputri interchangeably throughout the rest of this chapter because she is the protector of all living beings: humans, animals, birds, trees, and everything else–including you and me. As someone who never felt safe or protected growing up, I loved learning about Shailputri and have come to think of her as a protector who always has my back when I face trials and tribulations. A true friend, she is solid like a tree, and I can depend on her fully and forever.

## STABILITY & THE FIRST CHAKRA

The power of stability is connected with the first chakra (known as the "root chakra"). Its location is said to be the base of your spine. This is where spiritual energy is activated, and it rises upward from here toward the highest chakras, where it leads to the ultimate experience of enlightenment. This first (root) chakra is associated with the earth element and the sense of smell. Cultivating the power of stability by balancing this first chakra brings you the gift of great health, along with a solid foundation to be able to continue to progress along your spiritual journey.

Shailputri is depicted riding a bull, which represents the weighty stability of her grounded-ness. She carries a lotus flower. And a beautiful way to visualize your root chakra is as the roots of a lotus. In Eastern wisdom traditions, the lotus is a powerful symbol of the awakening of your spiritual power. For the lotus of spiritual knowledge to bloom in your life, you have to ensure its roots are planted firmly in the ground. In your body, you want to feel steady at your base, to cultivate strong and stable "roots," so your energy can then rise to higher chakras.

# Taking Inventory

For most of my life, I was nothing like Shailputri. By the time I had finished college and begun working in marketing communications in New York, I felt depleted from a lifestyle that had me going 24/7. Everything that was supposed to give me peace, comfort, and joy no longer worked. I knew that I needed a change, and I frequently longed for some sort of rebirth even though I wasn't quite sure what that meant.

I first spent six months studying Yoga and Ayurveda in India, and then I moved to California and began teaching Yoga and meditation to young people in juvenile detention centers. For almost two years, I focused on healing others and repressed my own pain with negative coping strategies that frequently made things worse. Although I saw that I moved others through my teaching, I was in hiding, not only from myself and others but also from my parents, who disapproved of the pivot I had made from business to the nonprofit world.

Prior to creating and beginning this practice in earnest, I had made a pilgrimage across the U.S., Spain, Australia, and India looking for answers to my challenges. I could not sleep at night, had trouble digesting my food, and suffered from mysterious aches and pains as well as lots of anxious, racing thoughts. Even though I didn't know it at the time, having an imbalanced root chakra means you regularly experience much of what I did. Fear, anxiety, and flashbacks can affect more than your mind. Physically, an imbalanced root chakra can give you issues with your colon, bladder, and bowels as well as lower back pain and discomfort in your legs or feet. Eating disorders are a strong sign of root chakra imbalances. A general feeling of insecurity can also indicate that your root chakra needs balancing.

Like me, you may know that you need to do things differently, that your old patterns no longer serve you, and that dabbling in new, healthier habits isn't ever really going to get you where you want to be. As the process of change began for me, I longed for something deeper, something that would provide meaning and structure, something that would enable me to live a life of purpose without abandoning myself in the process. Whether consciously or subconsciously, I returned to Navratri and to the power of the goddesses that I had celebrated during my childhood.

The first step was to take inventory of myself, to look in the mirror so that I could really see myself, both the positive and the negative. Perhaps you know the feeling, as you shuffle through your own life experiences, looking for a time or even a moment in which you felt whole. You might be spending far more energy than you'd like pretending away negative or even traumatic experiences or feelings that you know you must face. Perhaps you're looking to the future and hoping to be happier with yourself, in relationships and at work, but you're not quite sure how to begin that process. In this chapter, I will show you how.

Questions to consider when you're taking inventory around cultivating the power of stability:

1. What kinds of activities make me feel out of control (procrastinating, talking too much, drinking alcohol, taking drugs, watching too much television, scrolling Instagram one too many times, overexercising, traveling a lot, etc.)?

2. When I do activities that make me feel out of control, how do I feel physically and emotionally?

3. How would I feel if I had more stability in my life?

4. Is there some kind of pain that being all over the place is helping me avoid? Can I name it to begin to tame it?

5. How could developing more stability in my life benefit me in terms of my health and spiritual journey?

# Starting a Practice

Without a physical, practical grounding, it's hard to tap into your spiritual being to do the quiet, hard work of knowing and trusting the wisdom of your own soul. You already have everything you need to heal yourself. Once you begin to tune in to the sound of your inner voice, Goddess Shailputri can speak to and comfort you, as she does to me. It's a matter of trusting yourself and believing that the majestic beauty and power of the goddess Shailputri lives inside you.

If you've ever tried to start something new, you know how difficult it can be to make it a consistent habit. Yet, when you stick to a spiritual or wellness practice, the practice itself supports you in overcoming both mind and body challenges and can help you evolve spiritually. What follows is my process for starting and integrating the kinds of new practices that have been extremely helpful for me in deepening my own wellness.

### *Set an intention and write it down.*

Whenever I do this, I often stare at a blank page for some period of time until inspiration arrives. Once your intention has come to you and you have written it down, return to it by reading and rereading it often.

Setting intentions in writing has been one of the most potent tools for personal transformation in my life. Whenever I write my intentions, I find I receive opportunities in my life to actualize them. Usually this means I am confronted with the exact challenges I need to consistently surrender to the power of my intention, to overcome the obstacles on my path.

When I finally decided enough was enough, I set a *sankalpa*, or resolved intention, to:

> Find the strength to let go of what needs to be let go,
> The courage to reclaim what needs to be reclaimed
> And the wisdom to hold on to only that which is eternal
> and changeless.

I had no idea how I was going to go about finding the strength I knew I needed to heal and free myself from my past trauma. I simply knew I was determined to do whatever it took, so I surrendered before the goddess in my heart and declared, "I'm ready."

### Reach out for support.

It is a brave decision to embark upon an inward journey, so if there is anyone who encourages you to live your best life, reach out to them to share your intentions. In my organization's online programs, we assign every student a community buddy so that no matter how scared they might feel, they are never alone in their quest.

The day I proclaimed to the universe my readiness to heal myself, I felt extremely vulnerable. Until then, I had rarely discussed my own painful experiences, but that day, I shared my life story with my friend Mitchell. I had always been the rock upon which my friends and communities relied, and I often held space for and listened compassionately to others. But that day, I gave myself permission to receive compassionate deep listening, and I felt so supported by Mitchell's kindness. By the time he dropped me off at my apartment that night, I had begun to sense a new strength inside.

### Retreat inward.

It doesn't matter if you are working a full-time job when you begin to take on the practice of grounding yourself. What retreating inward means is saying no to unnecessary things in your life, such as extra work, social engagements, and travel. It also means carving out time for solitude, even if only for ten to fifteen minutes each day. This time gives you space to focus on rewiring your patterns.

It was important for me to withdraw from teaching so I could become a better student. I saved enough money to take a month off from work before figuring out a new way to earn a living that would allow more flexibility in my daily schedule.

I limited my outside interactions to just a couple of phone calls and one social engagement toward the end of the month. Having extended periods of silence felt intimidating initially. How I longed for something to fill that silence! But I resisted the urge to distract myself with noise, and eventually, the prolonged period of silence and solitude was what gave me the safe space I needed to feel my fear, anger, sadness, guilt, and regret at all the ways I had harmed myself over the years by neglecting myself.

### Feel all your feelings.

This is such an important part of spiritual transformation, to ensure that the practices you adopt will support your evolution and to prevent bypassing the emotional aspect of transformation. Tears are incredibly cleansing and therapeutic. Feelings must be acknowledged, embraced, and ideally released through sacred tears.

The thunderous, intense sobbing I did during these initial months of change felt liberating. I continued to peel back layers of fear, doubt, confusion, and anxiety by writing. I gave myself permission to write freely, in a stream-of-consciousness flow. I wrote down memories. I recorded flashbacks of painful experiences when I felt violated and feared for my life. This naturally led to more crying. Instead of holding back tears to avoid making others uncomfortable, I, in my aloneness, gave myself space for the tears to flow. And they did. Abundantly.

### Apply the practice.

Merely gathering knowledge does not bring about a transformation in your life. It is possible to read spiritual books, hear inspiring spiritual lectures, and even write spiritual books and give spiritual lectures and still not actually be spiritual.

To apply a practice, you may need to, as a first step, invest in some new equipment like foods, spices, herbs, oils, an alarm clock, pens, or paper. You will also need to spend time reflecting on practical steps you need to take to apply a practice. For example, if you endeavor to go to bed earlier so you can wake up earlier, consider the activities and distractions that keep you up late. Can you begin those tasks earlier in the day or eliminate them altogether? If cooking sounds intimidating, what tools (like an Instant Pot) can you invest in to make the process easier? Spending time on these practical, logistical questions will help you to prepare.

In my own case, one of the first decisions I made was to begin eating food that better nourished me. That meant throwing away whatever junk food remained in my pantry. I got rid of salsa-flavored chips, pretzels, and other once-tantalizing snacks, removing temptations in order to lay the groundwork for new habits. Eating more nourishing foods helped me feel much more physically and mentally grounded so that I could look deeper within and see the traumas I had experienced in my life through a more empowering lens.

## Application equals power.

Application equals power. Applying what you've learned in the laboratory of your own life is how you transform knowledge into wisdom and power, by proving the teachings with your own personal experience.

As Buddha once revealed:

" Do not believe what you have heard.

Do not believe in tradition because it is handed down many generations.

> Do not believe because the written statements come from some old sage.
>
> Do not believe in conjecture.
>
> Do not believe in authority or teachers or elders.
>
> But after careful observation and analysis, when it agrees with reason and it will benefit one and all, then accept it and live by it. 🙶

When you apply knowledge, it becomes your own. Once the profound truths of life manifest in your every thought, word, and action, you lead a spiritual life. This kind of life sets you free.

### Be consistent.

Spiritual growth is measured by the stability of your mind. Stability arises with consistency. It takes consistent, persistent effort to be stable in body and mind so you can feel your spiritual strength and power. Before you choose a practice or two, reflect on how you may be able to continue it consistently. Fortunately, many of the practices I share in this chapter (and in this book!) take fewer than fifteen minutes. And many take only three to five minutes!

You may also even find that doing these practices opens up time in your life to add more of what you love to do, by increasing the quality of *sattva* (mental clarity, purity, and peacefulness) in your daily existence. Many times, when we have more *rajas* (mental agitation and stress due to doing too much, too fast) and *tamas* (mental inertia that makes us feel stuck, inactive, confused, and conflicted), we accomplish less than we might if our minds were calm and composed. As you do these practices, the increased sense of calm you feel will support you in taking a balanced amount of action, with a clear and focused mind.

The best way to describe my one-month spiritual retreat was as an intense rebirth. Every time I pushed against my resistance to practice, I felt heroic. Every time I allowed myself to feel my emotions without trying to block them, I felt relief. Each victory propelled me to more victories. Even though I still felt so much pain inside and my vulnerabilities were ever present, I could feel myself transforming into a spiritual warrior.

To make way for the new, we need to let go of and destroy the old, much like Shailputri did when she was consumed by the inner fire of her desire for a new life. This is how the process of ego purification takes place. In addition to a lotus flower, Shailputri carries a trident. The three prongs of her trident represent the three divine powers of creation, maintenance, and destruction. These are all relevant at the beginning of a new undertaking, like starting your spiritual journey. To create something new, you must also let go of and even destroy parts of your past that no longer serve you, so you can make space to create and maintain a healthy new life. This includes new thoughts, beliefs, and values you want to adopt, habits you want to cultivate, and a lifestyle you want to create, all of which unfold throughout your journey with this book and begin with the power of stability.

## The Path Forward: Practices for Stability

The grounding practices in this section help you to balance your first (root) chakra by building a healthy earth element in your body, which then translates to a healthier mind, since the body and mind are so deeply interconnected. Goddess Shailputri is also known as Mother Earth, so all these practices help you restore your connection with nature as your own mother who can nurture and care for you when you align yourself with her eternal rhythms.

A great teacher in nature during seasons of instability and uncertainty is the mountain, which is full of the earth element embodied by Goddess Shailputri. "Solid as a rock" is a great way to describe the earth. You can also see the sturdiness of the earth in the grounded nature of trees, the hardness of nuts, and the rooted quality of vegetables that grow underground. In your body, the earth element expresses itself in your skin, bones, nails, teeth, hair, and tendons.

Earth element gives you the power of perseverance, which translates into stability and a sense of grounding in your root chakra. The following first-chakra balancing practices will give you stability and help you awaken to the power of Goddess Shailputri.

### PRACTICE: *Thank Goddess Shailputri each morning to connect with Mother Earth.*

There is a special mantra of gratitude toward Goddess Shailputri, our beautiful Mother Earth, that you can simply remember or chant when you wake up each morning. Mantras are like spiritual medicine that helps you overcome draining repetitive thoughts, so you can be more stable and present in each moment. The word *mantra* itself literally comes from two Sanskrit words: *tra*, which means "to protect," and *man*, the "thinking mind."

I love chanting this mantra before stepping my foot onto the ground. The meaning of the gratitude mantra to Mother Earth acknowledges Nature as Goddess Shailputri, who "has the ocean as her garment and mountains as her breasts. We ask for forgiveness for touching you with our feet."

*Samudra vasane devi [pronounced samu-DRA vas-NEY day-vi]*

*Parvata stana mandale [PAR-vata stana MUN-duley]*

*Vishnu patni namastubhyam [VISH-nu pat-NI na-MAS-tu-bhi-UM]*

*Paada sparsham kshama-svame [PAA-da spar-SHUM sha-MA-sva-MAY]*

The goal of Yoga is a sacred union of your individual Self with the universe. When you acknowledge your interconnectedness with Goddess Shailputri as Mother Nature each day in simple ways, like even saying "Thank you, Mother Earth" before stepping your foot onto the ground, you move toward a deeper connection with Mother Nature and all her creatures, large and small. Gratitude is the opposite of fear, anxiety, and insecurity. Giving thanks each day reframes destabilizing thoughts and phobias into optimism, contentment, and a profound sense of grounding that really balances your root chakra.

### PRACTICE: *Stop and smell the marigolds for instant calm and stability.*

Activating your sense of smell is a simple and easy way to ease anxiety, fear, and worries. Stopping to smell the marigolds has a stabilizing effect on your mind, helping you come back into the present moment. Roses, marigolds, and jasmine flowers have scents that are said in ancient texts to soothe and evoke mental clarity and stability. I love to picture Goddess Shailputri amidst the scent of such flowers while inhaling their aroma to balance my first chakra.

### PRACTICE: *Embody Goddess Shailputri in Mountain Pose.*

Standing in Mountain Pose is a simple grounding practice, especially if you are dealing with a lot of anxiety and insecurity. Starting your mornings in Mountain Pose can help you face the unpredictability of the day with steadiness and stability, like the majestic goddess Shailputri, especially when you approach the practice with this intention.

Connect with Mother Earth from the ground up. Close your eyes while standing and visualize a mountain and how stable it is. You can then affirm that "I am stable as a mountain" and "I am secure inside myself." The affirmations and posture connect with the spirit of Goddess Shailputri, residing steadfast in your first chakra.

Then really root your feet into the ground, standing tall, firm, and strong, with shoulders back. Fix your gaze at the horizon. Or look into your own eyes in a mirror. Breathe deeply for several breaths until you feel more confident, stable, and strong.

## PRACTICE: *Experience Goddess Shailputri's stability in Tree Pose.*

Tree Pose is an excellent practice to root and balance your first chakra, as well as to stabilize your legs and feet (any discomfort in these areas of your body is a definite sign of first chakra imbalance). Studies have shown that the practice of Tree Pose has positive effects on overall balance, stability, and physical coordination.

Begin in Mountain Pose (see prior practice for description). Close your eyes here and imagine your favorite tree. It could be a tree you used to climb during childhood. I personally love to imagine the bodhi tree, under which the Buddha gained enlightenment. Though I have not yet seen it in real life, its large roots and widespread branches suggest comfort and security.

Trees inspire because they are stable, rooted firmly in the earth. As you plant one foot in the ground, feel yourself rooting more deeply into the earth. Imagine that you are as grounded as Goddess Shailputri, that nothing can shake your resolve. From this place of inner resolution, slowly lift your opposite leg and place your foot on your standing leg, either below or above your knee, but never right on your knee.

Keep your hands pressed together, with your thumbs touching your heart, then extend your hands above your head. As you stand on one leg, contemplate how you can be like Goddess Shailputri and live with greater resolve to know your true Self.

**PRACTICE:** *Root into Mother Earth with your feet.*

You can awaken to Goddess Shailputri through the soles of your feet–one of the main locations of the root chakra. This stabilizing practice is calming for anyone feeling unstable, anxious, or insecure. Spending time in nature is often the best way to bring about a sense of refuge, security, and protection.

Take off your shoes and walk in nature, ideally near a body of water, such as the ocean, a lake, river, or stream. As you walk barefoot, feel the connection between the soles of your feet and the ground beneath them. Sink your feet even deeper. Close your eyes if you can and allow the stabilizing energy of Goddess Shailputri's manifestation as Mother Earth to calm your worries and fears as it brings balance to your root chakra through your feet.

## Allow yourself to slow down.

Allow yourself to slow down. Experiment by making your footsteps as light as you can, barely touching the surface of the sand, dirt, or grass. Then see how it feels to press down firmly, perhaps planting yourself in one spot for some time. Breathe deeply through your nose. Experience the freedom of traveling, however long or briefly, without distractions. Leave your phone inside–or turn it off. Unplug from the outer world and plug into your inner world, where Goddess Shailputri resides.

**PRACTICE:** *Oil your feet before bedtime for sound sleep.*

Oiling your feet before sleep is an excellent stability-enhancing practice, especially if you suffer from headaches, light-headedness, insomnia, or nightmares. Because your feet are full of subtle energy centers (called *marma* points in Ayurveda) that relieve insomnia and stress, oiling your feet before bedtime helps you get the deepest, least disturbed sleep possible.

Warm up sesame oil (in cold seasons) or coconut oil (in warm seasons), and then rub it into your feet. Make sure to do so slowly to relieve stress and tension in your feet. Massage between each of your toes; really press on the soles of your feet and move in a circular motion around your ankle joints.

*Sneha* is a Sanskrit word that means "to oil." *Sneha* also means "to love," making this a beautiful practice to awaken the love of Goddess Shailputri in the soles of your feet.

### PRACTICE: *Establish a healthier sleep schedule.*

When we talk about awakening the goddess Shailputri within you, the literal act of waking up (and going to sleep) in a rhythmic way is beneficial not only for your physical stability but also for your spiritual evolution. One sign of an imbalanced root chakra is insomnia. Not being able to fall asleep or sleep throughout the night affects your energy level during the day. It also affects your digestion.

When you wake up early and go to bed early (ideally by six A.M. and ten P.M., respectively), you can fall asleep and stay asleep more easily than at other times. This sleep cycle also stabilizes your digestion and ensures easier elimination in the morning, making the practice especially helpful for those who suffer from constipation. It also awakens a quality of the mind that is peaceful, clear, calm, and stable (known as *sattva* in Sanskrit).

Sleep itself is described in ancient wisdom texts as Shailputri—a mothering goddess who stabilizes your being from the inside out. When you (ideally) wake up before the sun, you can witness the transition from darkness to light, which is symbolic of the spiritual journey of enlightenment you embark upon during Navratri. Waking up early boosts your spirit. In ancient times, yogis and meditators all arose early to perform spiritual practices, as predawn is considered the most sacred and auspicious time of the day to remember the divinity that lives within you.

If waking up with the sun is a huge adjustment for you, transition your body clock gradually, in fifteen-minute intervals, so you can eventually sleep by ten P.M. and wake up by six A.M. Ancient holistic wisdom suggests this will ensure the best possible quality of sleep, which will keep your immune system strong, support your digestion, and help you receive spiritual insights.

PRACTICE: **Soak in Mother Moon's stabilizing rays.**

Lunar energy is feminine, goddess energy, whereas solar energy is more active and masculine. The moon's energy helps to calm your mind and body, enhancing feelings of receptivity, softness, serenity, and comfort. Soaking in the moon's rays is a way of absorbing Goddess Shailputri's nurturing, grounding, maternal presence. Take a walk in the moonlight, or if possible, sit or even sleep under the moonlight as an excellent antidote to anxiety, overthinking, overreacting, stress, fear, and worry.

PRACTICE: **Eat more grounding foods as an offering to Goddess Shailputri.**

When you consider that your body is your temple, the kinds of foods you offer it become important for your spiritual practice, as well as your physical and mental stability. If you consider that Goddess Shailputri lives within you, you want to eat stabilizing foods that awaken you to her power of stability.

There are three types of foods in Yoga philosophy. *Inertia-inducing foods* make balancing your first chakra and awakening to Goddess Shailputri within you nearly impossible. *Agitating foods* increase your anxiety, instability, and insecurity. *Pure foods* help you connect with the goddess within and balance your first chakra. You want to eat fewer inertia-inducing and agitating foods and consume more grounding pure foods for overall stability.

Foods that are canned, processed, and frozen are inertia inducing. Eating excessive meat (especially beef and pork, which tend to sit in your stomach and make it hard for you to move after eating) and even mushrooms and certain cheeses (like blue cheese) also create lethargy and make you feel sluggish. These foods also tend to cause constipation.

Agitating foods are those that make you feel anxious, nervous, worried, and scared. Agitating foods include hot, burning spices like chili sauces, excessive garlic, ginger, black pepper, and other pungent spices. These foods can lead to digestive disturbances like loose stools, constipation, or alternating diarrhea and constipation, all of which destabilize your root chakra.

Pure foods give you physical and mental stability. I always feel that I am making a sacred offering to Goddess Shailputri when I eat pure foods, which are full of *prana* (yogic "life force") and are seasonal. You can find seasonal foods in local farmers' markets or community-supported agriculture (CSA) organizations. Organic seasonal vegetables and fruits give your body strength and stability. Lightly cooking seasonal vegetables and grains with ghee (clarified butter) and fragrant, gentle spices like cumin, fennel seeds, and turmeric adds to their ability to provide nutrition that enhances stability, awakens Goddess Shailputri, and balances the first chakra.

Each of these practices is an opportunity for connecting with the power of stability that Goddess Shailputri symbolizes. From here, this grounding and purification will serve as the foundation for the remainder of your spiritual journey of Navratri.

**Chapter 2**

# Channeling Your Energy

*What's like nectar in the beginning becomes like poison in the end.*
*What's like poison in the beginning becomes like nectar in the end.*

—BHAGAVAD GITA, chapter 18, verses 37–38

## Cultivating Creativity

When you hear the word *creativity*, you may immediately think of painting, writing, or another artistic pursuit, but from a spiritual perspective, the idea of creativity represents something more intimate and personal. Within the nine-part journey of Navratri, creativity describes the energy you need to create (or re-create) yourself and consciously craft the kind of life you hope to lead. If you've taken the first step toward becoming grounded on day 1 of the Navratri practice, the next step is to consider how you're spending your energy.

The Vedic spiritual tradition is built on the foundation of *brahmacharya*, which in practice refers to abstaining from sex but also means following the path that leads to experiencing *Brahman* (higher consciousness, or your own divine Self). The practice of abstinence can be applied in many settings, like refraining from eating foods that are harmful for you, taking screen breaks, or pausing from toxic relationships. The process of detachment from these sensory experiences and our desires for them begins with a period of abstinence from the very thing we want most, a period that allows us to recalibrate and determine with a clear head how to move forward.

A Vedic astrologer once described the man I was destined to marry and when I would meet him. The man, to my amazement, did come into my life when the astrologer said he would, but other Vedic astrologers I consulted later predicted I would have divorced him. I told him during our passionate, short-lived relationship that I wanted to deepen my brahmacharya, something I had intuitively practiced more easily before meeting him. Even though I physically enjoyed being with him, my soul was not pleased, as he transgressed my physical boundaries, drank a lot of alcohol, and could not control his explosive rage, which he took out on me. As a survivor of sexual abuse, I knew I needed to untangle myself from this relationship to continue to heal myself from past sexual abuse and to walk the path of realizing Brahman, my true Self.

Although brahmacharya involves regulating all your senses, it focuses intensely on sexuality, as all the senses are involved in the sexual act, and it is therefore considered the most difficult to control. One ancient Ayurvedic text advises that you should have sexual relations only with someone you approve of mentally, someone who engages in respectful speech, lives by ethical values, is not sexually demanding, and honors healthy boundaries. My experience with this man and the realization that I was with someone harmful to me inspired me to turn even more deeply inward. Although I had been practicing brahmacharya before I met him, the practice had been theoretical. Only after our relationship did I realize how strong sexual attraction could truly be and how difficult it is to control, even if a connection with someone else is not good for you.

Instead of pursuing the relationship, I developed a passionate affair with my higher Self. I went deep into applying Ayurveda and Yoga to honor my body as the abode of Goddess Brahmacharini, who is inviolable to any kind of abuse. I channeled my sexual energy into writing articles and books, and I pioneered the introduction of Ayurveda into prestigious universities, prisons, and more. When this man and I separated, the practice of brahmacharya helped me purify my relationship with him such that I could let go of him with love (for good) when we crossed paths five years after I first broke up with him. I discovered, as so many before me had, that brahmacharya is the foundation of my strength. It helped me overcome deep trauma, connect with my purpose, and see divinity in myself and in all beings.

Whether you are facing similar challenges reclaiming your energy after experiences of abuse or want to detach from less traumatic but also significant sensory distractions that prevent you from living your purpose, you can turn to Goddess Brahmacharini to help you achieve a state of purification that will provide a deeper connection to your own true power.

## Knowing BRAHMACHARINI

The legend of Brahmacharini is a complicated one that illustrates the challenges of using traditional wisdom in a modern setting. Yet, if we can understand the story symbolically versus literally, I believe it offers many lessons about reclaiming our power.

After immolating herself, Shailputri was reborn as Brahmacharini, daughter of the spiritual king of the Himalayan Mountains. She was determined to marry Lord Shiva again in her new life, so she dedicated herself to the practice of brahmacharya, "the path of self-control." For one thousand years, she ate only fruits and flowers. For the next hundred years, she ate only vegetables. Then, for three thousand years, she ate leaves that fell from trees. She slept on the forest floor under the vast open sky for years on end to demonstrate the discipline that empowered

her to identify with her true Self. By the end of the story, she even gave up eating fallen leaves.

The news of such great discipline reached far and wide. Lord Brahma, father of the sage Narada, appeared before her. "No one has performed brahmacharya the way you have. The only way you could have undertaken all these difficulties was due to true and pure love for Lord Shiva. May you be blessed with Lord Shiva as your husband in this birth as well."

While this may sound like an extreme–and even scary–story, I don't see it as the tale of a goddess who gave up everything to marry a god. Instead, I understand it as the story of a Truth seeker who gave up all distractions to merge with the ultimate Truth. The story of Brahmacharini and Shiva is not meant to be the story of a romantic relationship; Shiva is merely symbolic of the true Self. He is pure consciousness, the eternal soul, which we strive to merge with vis-à-vis the power of spiritual practice.

Gods and goddesses may be endowed with superhuman abilities, like living off air, but this is only to illustrate, through hyperbole, the intensity of the spiritual discipline required to know your true Self. That's because only when we are established in our true Self, can we really know and love another's true Self, and thereby experience the bliss of true union.

I thought of Goddess Brahmacharini's story often during the nine years of intense spiritual disciplines I practiced while learning this knowledge. I willingly gave up boyfriends and sensual pleasures during this time to learn how to discern which people and projects were worthy of my time and attention. It was a long, difficult, solitary journey.

Over the years, Brahmacharini gave me the strength to undergo the process of purification, to navigate all the emotions that arise in partnerships without losing myself in them. That is the power of brahmacharya.

# CREATIVITY & THE SECOND CHAKRA

The power of creativity is related to the second (sacral) chakra, located in the area of your reproductive organs. It is connected with sexuality (the power to create new human beings), your emotions, creative projects, and ideas. The second chakra is associated with the water element and the sense of taste. It flows. There is a watery aspect of sexuality, in terms of sexual fluids that are responsible for the spark of new creation. Each of your emotions too, which you experience with the watery saliva on your tongue, can be seen as a flavor. Love is the ultimate sweet taste. Some experiences leave a sour taste in your mouth. At times, we feel bitter. Or the fiery pungency of anger and rage. Cultivating the ability to channel the wild waves of your emotional and sexual energy into creative and constructive outlets is the power of creativity that a balanced second chakra brings.

Brahmacharini supports you in the endless ocean of emotion. She carries a *japa mala*, or rosary of prayer beads, in one of her hands. And a *kalash*, a small copper vessel that holds water, in the other. These beautiful objects are weapons to support you on the spiritual journey of self-mastery. The japa mala helps you focus your energy on a single mantra that you traditionally repeat 108 times (one mantra per bead) to channel your energy into the positivity of the words of the mantra. The kalash represents the potential of the water element to cleanse and bless your whole being even if your emotions and sexuality become muddy and confusing.

# Taking Inventory

Learning that Goddess Brahmacharini lives in my second chakra gave me a feeling of safety and protection I had never had before. The Sanskrit term for the second chakra, *svadhishthana*, means "one's own abode." Knowing that a goddess lives in my second chakra taught me to value my inner home and sexuality as a sacred power, to be offered only to a person worthy of it. This is the meaning of brahmacharya, the path of channeling your sexual energy into the spiritual journey of knowing your true Self and exercising the discernment to keep sexual expression a sacred one.

There are many benefits to brahmacharya practice. One is the tremendous willpower and self-control you gain. Brahmacharya heightens your creativity and strengthens the mental and physical stability that Goddess Shailputri in the first chakra provides. It improves your complexion and gives you a more magnetic personality. The famous spiritual leader Swami Vivekananda had amazing magnetism from a lifetime of brahmacharya. At a physiological level, the ancient wisdom of Ayurveda reveals that abstinence from sex helps rebuild your immunity. As sexual tissue is interlinked with your overall immunity, or *ojas* per Ayurveda, the less you lose this tissue through orgasm, the stronger your sexual tissue and, hence, overall health. One of the greatest benefits of brahmacharya practice is the mental discernment it provides, giving us the strength to practice detachment.

But the concept of brahmacharya goes far beyond sex. We can also think of it as the right use of energy. The practice of brahmacharya represents movement toward a balanced, distraction-free space, in which we minimize or eliminate distractions from behaviors that cause us to eat too little or too much, listen to overly loud music, smell unpleasant odors, or any other sensory experience that prevents us from achieving equilibrium in daily life.

The first step of brahmacharya practice is awareness. To achieve sensory awareness, you can take inventory of your senses by asking yourself these questions:

1. Am I under- or overusing my eyes? Do I have too much screen time? Do I suppress my need to sleep and keep my eyes forcefully open for too many hours of the day? Do I absorb violent images or anything else disturbing?

2. Am I eating too little or too much? Am I eating healthy foods? Do I self-soothe with unhealthy foods? Do I avoid eating to punish myself?

3. How often am I aware of my sense of smell? When I begin noticing the scents around me, are they pleasant or unpleasant?

4. What sounds do I hear regularly? Do I have enough silence in my life? Do I use my sense of hearing to listen to gossip, arguments, and yelling? Do I hear enough sounds of nature?

5. Do I receive too much or too little touch? Do I crave physical contact? Do I overindulge in physical contact, including sex? Do I hurt myself by cutting or otherwise inflicting pain on my body?

## Channeling Your Creativity/Energy

Once you know the answers to these questions, you will be in a better position to regulate yourself. Though all our threads of energy combine into sexual energy, brahmacharya practice not only addresses sexuality but also the individual energetic channels that combine to create it. By understanding our own sensory needs, we can put ourselves on the path to knowing ultimate Truth and experiencing the world and ourselves in healthy ways that allow us to let go of old habits and behaviors and welcome new ones.

The challenges I faced in my life, along with the awareness that Goddess Brahmacharini lives in my second chakra, helped me as I began my own practice of brahmacharya. Until then, my sexuality felt like something out of my control that caused me pain, suffering, and fear. But actively choosing brahmacharya made me feel powerful in a way I had never felt before, and I came to understand that no matter how much trauma I had previously experienced, I was–and am–pure, no matter what.

**Identify the sensory experiences in your life that bring you clarity and peace of mind, as well as those that do not.**

Humans are pleasure-seeking creatures, but the unbounded pursuit of pleasure, of "nectar" in the words of the Gita, can backfire and become poison without awareness and detachment. If you've taken inventory of the primary sensory experiences in your life, you can now go further and classify those experiences as *tamasic* (unconscious and inertia inducing), *rajasic* (stimulating or agitating), or *sattvic* (purity and clarity promoting). Ideally, you will begin this process with one or two areas in which your sensory experiences are sattvic, but even if that's not the case, it's okay. The process of brahmacharya is designed to purify your life in preparation for transformation. At the beginning, removing harmful experiences is more important than adding more sattvic ones.

In my case, I identified that my food and lifestyle habits, three years into my spiritual journey, gave me tremendous peace and clarity of mind. My boyfriend's presence, however, did not. Though I broke up with him shortly after that realization, I had a hell of a time getting him out of my mind. It was only when I identified our relationship as rajasic, or agitating, that I could start moving forward.

**Determine, as best you can, whether unhealthy relationships with people and objects of the senses serve a purpose in your life.**

Sometimes the limiting thoughts, behaviors, and feelings in our lives serve a purpose, while at other times, we may simply be pursuing practices that aren't good for us out of habit and lack of awareness. Either way, the second step of a brahmacharya practice is to create awareness of the drive behind your desires. At the beginning, you may not have a clear answer, but the cyclical practice of Navratri will allow you to revisit these questions at regular intervals. You may need time to consider and understand yourself, especially if this process awakens difficult or painful truths.

Because I had practiced self-control with men I had been attracted to in the past, I had never truly realized how deep and intense sexual desires could be. This was an important experience, as it helped me empathize with the pain others go through due to sexual attraction, something I honestly did not understand as well before, given my previous ascetic inclinations. I had to rely on every ounce of strength I had to pull away from my ex-boyfriend in spite of my newfound insight that it was not a healthy relationship.

Before I cut ties with him, my ex-boyfriend showed me how much anger, fear, and shame I had from unresolved childhood sexual traumas. If it were not for my unhealthy relationship with him, I may not have known just how many issues I still had to resolve within myself. Though it was painful at the time, I ultimately feel that his presence in my life served an important purpose.

**Choose a higher ideal to anchor yourself in.**
It is impossible to give up anything. Per the ancient Vedic spiritual teachings, we can only *take up* something higher, desire-wise, which causes us to drop our lower desires, like a young adult automatically drops a childhood fascination for toys when, for example, discovering a desire for higher education.

The ideal that anchored me in the practice of brahmacharya was Self-realization. I truly wanted to know my deepest Self. In deepening my brahmacharya practice after breaking up with my boyfriend, I deepened my relationship with Brahmacharini and changed my view of myself,

from survivor of sexual trauma to warrior with an inviolable goddess living in my second chakra. Over time, I no longer saw sex as something to be scared of or ashamed about, but rather as a sacred experience of the divinity within, which must only be engaged in with someone else who shares that view. My short-lived experience of straying from brahmacharya with my ex-boyfriend taught me how important it is for someone to first open my heart before I give permission for them to enter my body.

After years of feeling objectified under the male gaze, I was finally able to achieve a new level of self-respect when I practiced brahmacharya. I began seeing myself as a divine being, and could see others as divine beings as well, even those who behaved badly. Though my ex-boyfriend hurt me, I still kept him in my heart for five years as I continued my spiritual journey and came to know my true Self.

Eventually, the practice of brahmacharya helped channel the human love I felt for him into the kind of divine love that the goddess Radha felt for Lord Krishna, who was her lover but never became her husband. If you remember from chapter 1, my mother and her friend dressed me as Radha for the goddess look-alike contest when I was a girl. Now, in addition to resembling Radha on the outside, I had achieved a degree of her inner strength on my spiritual journey.

**Choose new behaviors that align with your ideal.**
Once I set my ideal of Self-realization, I focused on learning everything I could about the Self. The three core values of the spiritual lineage within which I studied include *satsangha* (gathering around spiritual teachings that reflect Truth), *sadhana* (dedicated spiritual practice), and *seva* (selfless service).

I focused my energy on acts of service in the spiritual organization, ranging from meaningful tasks (like teaching or writing articles) to mundane ones (like cleaning the bathroom), to purify my ego and keep my mind focused. At first, the tedious tasks felt like drudgery, but that feeling began to shift when I edited a seventy-page document about the Gayatri Mantra, which is a prayer from a spiritual seeker to the divine sun (a symbol of the true Self within) to rise from the cloud of desires and reveal its effulgence. From then on, my experience of service and of japa mala and *Sandhya Vandanam*, the practices Goddess Brahmacharini performs to overcome the unconscious emotional patterns of the mind, became the tools I used daily to help me chip away at unconscious layers of my being.

With a deepened understanding of the meaning and value of the service I rendered and the spiritual practices I performed, brahmacharya started to become a beautiful nectar rather than the poison of deprivation. I felt a deep peace that I had never previously known. This fueled my spiritual and professional work in life-changing ways.

When my ex-boyfriend and I reconnected after five years of separation, he apologized and told me how much he still loved me. But because of the inner power I had developed from brahmacharya (which produced what he called an "alchemical change" in me), I was able to let go of him with love. My ex-boyfriend was so touched by the way I forgave him and said the love I had for him was like "seeing the face of God" and that my forgiveness of him was like "the beautiful fragrance violets give when crushed." I loved him enough to liberate him and free myself from codependency. What remains between us to this day is simply the pure love of the Self.

## The Path Forward: Practices for Creativity

I love how balanced the ancient Vedic spiritual tradition is in showing us the amazing path of abstinence alongside a beautiful, shame-free approach to sexuality as a divine experience. Pleasure is one of the four goals of human life in the ancient Vedas, which reveal that sexuality is an opportunity for both partners to experience a divine union with the divinity in one another (only once we experience our own divinity first). It is the highest joy we are blessed to experience as human beings at the physical level, provided we have a foundation firmly in place of knowing our own Self.

It is not about how much sex you have (although Ayurveda gives us very helpful seasonal guidance) but about approaching the act with respect for its sacredness. The more you focus on the bond between you and your partner, the more sex becomes an outward expression and communication of deep love and respect rather than a way to satisfy your needs vis-à-vis another person, who ends up being reduced to an object.

When I remember that Goddess Brahmacharini lives within me, I do not identify with my past. I am free from it. You too can heal from whatever holds you down from your past, when you gather the courage to face it with the power and self-mastery that brahmacharya practice provides to honor your sexuality in the realm of your own abode, the sacred second chakra.

## PRACTICE: *Master your mind with Goddess Brahmacharini's japa mala (rosary beads).*

Goddess Brahmacharini holds a japa mala (similar to a rosary) in one of her hands. It is one of the divine weapons used for the inner battle we must wage for self-mastery. You can silently or quietly repeat any mantra (set of inspiring words or affirmations) that you wish using the japa mala, which traditionally has 108 beads. The number 108 is a multiple of the number 9, which is the number of Navratri goddesses and the number of months of pregnancy.

To perform the japa mala practice, you simply chant one mantra of your choice per bead, and then move to the next bead on the left side. Every time your thoughts stray from your mantra, work to bring yourself back to being fully present. In the beginning, it helps to chant the mantra quietly to help you stay focused. Over time, as your concentration increases, you can do this practice internally.

My personal favorite mantra is the Gayatri Mantra (please refer to the appendix), which evokes the powers of the sun in our lives. Gayatri Mantra is the sacred sound of Goddess Durga. The word *gayatri* comes from the combination of the words *gaya*, meaning "poem," and *tri*, which means "three," and refers here to the combined power and strength of the three goddesses that represent different groupings of Durga's immense power: Kali, Lakshmi, and Saraswati.

In addition to being a collection of sacred sounds, Gayatri is a goddess who is an embodiment of the female form of the light of the sun (which is traditionally representative of masculine energy). Goddess Gayatri is worshipped for spiritual knowledge and wisdom, and the light of the sun symbolizes the divine wisdom that enlightens your soul.

Before embarking upon your battle for self-mastery vis-à-vis the japa mala practice, it helps to call upon support in the form of a witness. Your witness can be any form of divinity you connect most with. It could be the sun, moon, an animal, or even the vast, expansive sky. Perhaps Goddess Brahmacharini herself. Your witness can also be a human guide you have connected with who has taught or inspired you.

The japa mala practice helps to relax and control the mind so you can start to know your inner Self more intimately. I find this creativity-boosting practice deeply nurturing, soothing, and uplifting. Japa mala practice also helps pull your mind away from outer dependencies and draws you closer to your own inner strength and power.

### PRACTICE: *Cleanse yourself of attachments with the healing power of water.*

In addition to the japa mala, Goddess Brahmacharini holds a copper vessel called a kalash. There is an ancient spiritual cleansing practice with water from a kalash that evokes her power as well as that of all the goddesses. This exercise has helped me make huge leaps of faith and major transformations in my life by evoking the power of detachment. I practiced it daily for nine years, while immersed in full-time study of ancient Vedic spirituality. Nowadays, I love returning to it whenever I feel I need to cleanse myself of something occupying more space in my mind than is healthy.

This practice has helped me let go of anger, release shame, overcome fear, find my voice, and most of all, release myself from the grip of attachments to people, habits, and situations that brought emotional comfort but ultimately hindered my spiritual growth. A key part of this practice is identifying one to three things you want to let go of, and then symbolically releasing them with the cleansing and purifying power of water.

The name of this practice is Sandhya Vandanam, which means "prayer of thanksgiving" in Sanskrit. It is traditionally practiced before the sun rises during the transition period from darkness to light. We are the most vulnerable when we go through periods of transition and change. Hence, it helps tremendously to learn to hold on to the one thing that never changes (your own soul) as you practice letting go of what no longer serves you.

The core of the practice is a prayer for forgiveness of sin. It is fascinating that, in the Vedic tradition, there is no concept of original sin. Rather, sin is defined as any time you forget that your true identity is as an eternal soul, not as a body or mind. Whenever you identify with your body (like when you crave certain foods or sex) or with your mind (by holding on to negative thoughts and emotions like anger and fear), it is considered sin. Anything that takes you away from your true Self is sin. To cleanse ourselves from all the times we forget our true spiritual identity, we have this beautiful practice.

Instructions for practice:

1. Pour water into your kalash (copper vessel), or you can use any small vase you have.

2. Pour water from your vessel into the palm of one of your hands. Then you can use this water to cleanse your body (by drinking it from your hand) or simply sprinkle the water on top of your head to purify your being. Affirmation: "Knowledge in the form of Goddess Saraswati lives in me."

3. Repeat step 2 with the affirmation: "Abundance in the form of Goddess Lakshmi resides within my being."

4. Repeat step 2 with the affirmation: "Power in the form of Goddess Durga is my true essence."

5. Identify one thing you wish to let go of (e.g., anger, fear, jealousy, grief, frustration, attachment to someone or some situation). Then while pouring the water into one of your hands, imagine what you want to let go of. If it's a person, try to visualize their face. If it's an emotion, feel where and how you experience it in your body (in your heart, in the form of heat, etc.). Throw the water onto the ground and simultaneously imagine letting go of this visualization. (You may prefer to sit on a special towel for this practice if you have a wooden floor, for example.)

6. Repeat step 5 two more times. If you have only one main thing you are focused on letting go of, you can imagine yourself letting go of that thrice.

7. Now dip your fingers into your purifying vessel and bless each part of your body with the following affirmations (or ones you create on your own):
   a. "May my head be blessed with wisdom." Touch your fingers to the top of your head.
   b. "May my eyes be blessed to see the truth." Touch your fingers to your eyelids.

c. "May my ears be blessed to hear that which is auspicious." Touch your fingers to your ears.

d. "May my mouth be blessed to consume pure foods." Touch your fingers to your mouth.

e. "May my throat be blessed with divine speech." Touch your fingers to your throat.

f. "May my heart be blessed with purity." Touch your fingers to your heart.

g. "May my stomach be blessed to digest everything I come into contact with" (food, information, emotions, and life experiences). Touch your fingers to your navel.

h. "May my hands and feet be blessed to perform actions that bring about the greatest good for myself and others." Touch your fingers across your shoulders and arms and your feet and knees.

PRACTICE: *Channel your energy with the buzzing-bee breathing exercise.*

This simple yogic breathing exercise is a powerful way to close the doorways of the senses and go inward. It calms the nervous system, promotes focus, and supercharges your creativity. This breathing exercise is a wonderful way to channel your spiritual energy and to help you feel inspired and empowered from within, like Goddess Brahmacharini. It is fast and easy to do.

All *pranayamas* (breathing exercises) strengthen the intimate bond between the mind and the breath. When you calm and slow your breathing, your mind automatically becomes calmer and clearer. When you feel anxious and compulsive, you can observe how your breathing becomes strained. You may even notice how you hold your breath when you feel really attached to a person or situation.

I love practicing this breathing exercise to start my day in a more focused way. You can also practice this breathing exercise before sleep or anytime you feel anxious or just can't control your racing mind and obsessive desires.

Instructions for practice:

1. Place your thumbs inside your ears so you can hear only your own internal sound.

2. Gently cover your eyelids with your middle fingers, resting your index fingers upon your eyebrows.

3. Inhale through your nose.

4. Make a buzzing sound at your throat (like you would when humming) as you exhale. If done correctly, the sound of your humming will be the loudest sound you hear.

You can practice this once, three times, or as many times as you like provided you never feel dizzy doing it.

## PRACTICE: *Free yourself from sensual desires in Dhruvasana.*

Once upon a time, there was a prince named Dhruva who was destined to become a king. Unfortunately, his stepmother wanted her own biological son to be king, so she banished Dhruva to the forest for many years. Like Goddess Brahmacharini, Dhruva became deeply engaged in brahmacharya practices (like living on one meal a day, then only on fruits, then leaves, then finally living just on air). He gradually came to know who he was–his true Self–and was not dependent upon earthly things to survive.

Dhruva helped the queen and his half brother, who was now the king, to be stable in their kingdom. After some time, they brought him back to officially serve in his rightful position as the king. He said no. He didn't need dominion over the outer kingdom because he had realized through his journey of knowing his true Self that he had all the power and riches he needed within. He didn't need anything else.

The message of this story is that we have to let go of certain things to discover who we are deep inside and to be truly healthy. When I practice this yogic asana, I bring to my mind and heart one person I feel I cannot live without (or an outcome or other thing I feel attached to) and then imagine myself being completely free without them or it.

Attachment is the deepest root cause of psychological and emotional suffering. When innocent likes and dislikes turn into full-blown attachments, they can cause sorrow and eventually complete confusion and delusion. Our attachments entrap us. That is why one of my lineage teachers, Baba Ayodhya Nath, said: "Rise above wants. You have not come here to be chasing life's sprinkles, roses, and chocolate cake. You have come here to say [to your desires] 'get lost.' I am an emperor. I am eating apples and am content with the few simple clothes I have. When a hungry animal comes, I will give all my food or half my food and I will be so generous that soon I will find that there are five or ten people with me. And then you don't have to ask them why they are with you. They are with you because they are like you. You are all kings."

To practice Dhruvasana, bring your hands together, with both thumbs touching your heart. This *mudra* (yogic hand gesture) has a profoundly calming effect on the changeable nature of the mind.

Now stand on one leg with one foot on the inside of the opposite leg (either above or below the knee). Imagine yourself being fine without the one thing you are most attached to in life.

Connect with your heart. Experience freedom. Your true nature.

**PRACTICE:** *Abstain from sex–or your favorite sensual pleasure–for one week and channel your energy into creating something (art, writing, making something with your hands).*

Though it seems counterintuitive at first, abstinence brings about enjoyment. The more you can restrain your senses from going wild with enjoyment, the more you will be able to enjoy the same sensual experience when you do choose to indulge in it.

Imagine, for example, that you love vanilla ice cream. You crave it for days or even weeks, and then finally get to savor its sweet taste. The first ice cream cone is incredible. But then you may feel like having another. And then one more. And so on. By the time you get to the eighth ice cream cone, the ice cream may not taste so great. By the ninth or tenth cone, you may be repulsed by the same object that brought you such immense enjoyment at first!

When you channel your sexual energy into creative expression, you can experience increased inspiration, enthusiasm, imagination, insight, and the ability to sustain the creation of beautiful artwork, poetry, writing, music, and other forms of art. You start to connect with a deeper source of joy, which emerges from your higher Self, independent of anyone else.

Try it, and see how your creativity blossoms for even one week. You can abstain from sex or from any other sensual enjoyment, like your favorite food. Once you live without it, you will return to it with even greater enjoyment that comes from the spiritual practice of abstinence.

## PRACTICE: *Grow and use hibiscus flowers to support creative inspiration.*

Hibiscus flowers are called *japa kusum* in Sanskrit. *Japa* is the name of the practice of chanting mantras on a mala (rosary beads), as we explored earlier. The hibiscus is the favorite flower of Goddess Durga and has been used in sacred spiritual ceremonies for millennia in India. It is considered both physically purifying (when you consume it as a tea, which you can do by steeping its petals in hot water) and spiritually cleansing.

Hibiscus flowers, at a physiological level, help promote hair growth and clear skin. They support the healthy functioning of the kidneys and female reproductive system, which is why they have a deep connection with the second chakra.

In ancient cultures, flowers have deep spiritual significance and symbolism. The hibiscus flower represents feminine energy (which we all have, regardless of what gender we identify with). It is symbolic of the beauty and charm you become endowed with when you successfully practice brahmacharya.

Just as there are two sides to a balanced second chakra (either channeling your sexuality into something creative or expressing it in a sacred way), so too does the hibiscus flower have different meanings based on its color. White hibiscus flowers represent Brahmacharini's purity and beauty, the power of abstinence, and channeling your sexual energy into creative pursuits. Red hibiscus flowers, on the other hand, symbolize passion, true love, and divine romance.

You can wash your hair with hibiscus petals, drink hibiscus tea, or simply gaze at the flower itself to remember the goddess within, which is always pure and can never be violated.

### PRACTICE: *Eat your way to a healthier sexuality, immunity, and more sustained creativity.*

Eating foods to support a healthy sexuality is important whether or not you are sexually active. Your sexuality lives in every cell of your body. It is the most refined tissue of the body, created by the food you eat, according to ancient health wisdom of Ayurveda. The ancient Ayurvedic sages revealed the deep relationship between the health of your sexual tissue and overall immunity.

Sweet-tasting foods and foods with natural fats maximally support the health of your sexual tissue–provided you can digest them (by eliminating bowels once or twice each day with ease, ideally early in the morning). Digesting the naturally sweet foods helps endow you with fertility and immunity.

The best time of year to eat more naturally sweet foods is the winter season, from mid-November through mid-March. This is the time of year when your digestion is naturally strongest, and hence, you can eat more heavy foods to nourish yourself for the whole year ahead. Winter is also the time of year when you can eat the largest quantity of food. In the spring and summer, you are advised to eat less and lighter food as digestion steadily declines during this period.

## NATURALLY SWEET SEXUALITY- AND IMMUNITY-BOOSTING FOODS

| **Dairy:** ghee (clarified butter), cow's milk from well-treated cows, almond milk, coconut milk | **Fruits:** sweet mangoes, peaches, plums, pears, figs, bananas, pomegranates, raisins, dates, apricots |
|---|---|
| **Nuts:** almonds, walnuts, cashews | **Spices:** cloves, carom or ajwain seeds, turmeric, saffron, sesame seeds |

PRACTICE: *Use discernment when choosing a sexual partner.*

Remembering that Goddess Brahmacharini lives within you gives you the power to choose the best possible partner with whom to share your sexuality. It can't be just anyone. You must first discern that your potential partner is a worthy, noble person who respects you and honors healthy boundaries, and then determine whether this person also understands and appreciates the sacredness of sexuality. It is not enough for one partner to approach sexuality with a sense of reverence. Both partners must come with this same spiritual consciousness and intention for a divine experience of lovemaking for it to be truly so.

### PRACTICE: *Create a sacred sexual experience.*

The ancient Ayurvedic texts recommend first gaining physical strength from eating sweet aphrodisiac foods. They then advise engaging in sexual activity only when both partners are keenly interested and alone. Having sex if your own soul is not fully satisfied and ready is a form of self-betrayal. It is also important to have sex when you're feeling good and truly respect your partner.

You are recommended to indulge in sex when free from the urges to eat, drink, urinate, or eliminate the bowels. Sacred sexuality is recommended ideally at nighttime, at least two hours post-dinner. The second-best time is in the morning between six and ten A.M. The texts recommend looking and smelling beautiful for the sexual act by wearing cosmetics and even anointing yourself with wonderfully scented fragrances. Most important, rather than mindlessly enjoying the experience of sex, set an intention to connect with the divinity within yourself and your partner. This helps you approach the act of lovemaking as a profound kind of prayer, to awaken to the divine creative power that lives within. If you are trying to conceive a baby, it really helps to set an intention to welcome a new soul into both of your lives.

The ancient texts share recommendations to ensure you can regain lost strength and refresh yourself physically and mentally after the exertion of sexual intercourse. The primary recommendation for this is a recipe for warm, cooked almond milk (or whole milk from well-treated cows) with organic sugar (I personally use jaggery, which is an unrefined sugar), turmeric, and cardamom, which you can even prepare ahead of time. Keep the milk warm in a flask to drink afterward to immediately regain the sexual tissue that leaves your body with an orgasm. You are also advised to take a warm bath, wear fresh clothes, apply your favorite essential oils, and open a window or curtains and expose yourself to moonlight following sexual activity. All these practices help relieve exhaustion and restore calmness and clarity to your mind after the heat and passion of sexuality.

The freedom of spirit you'll start to experience when you embrace your body as your divine abode will ignite a new kind of joy within you that is kindled by restraint, sacred enjoyment, discernment, curiosity, and patience. When you give yourself the chance to withdraw from sensual stimulations, even for a short while, a deeper enjoyment of your sensuality becomes available to you with greater self-mastery over your own mind and emotions. This is the great gift of brahmacharya.

# Chapter 3

# Igniting the Fire of Transformation

*Just as one casting off worn-out garments puts on new ones, so the embodied casting off worn-out bodies enters new ones.*

—BHAGAVAD GITA, chapter 2, verse 22

## Cultivating Transformation

Transformation is not something that accidentally happens to us. Like every part of the Navratri cycle, it is something we initiate and experience again and again during our lives. For myself, day 3 of this cyclical practice (or week 3 or month 3, depending on how you structure your own Navratri practice) is an opportunity to do something outside my comfort zone. I use the energy I have collected from the day before to look fear in the face and challenge myself to go beyond what I have been capable of up until now.

There is a Sanskrit word, *kavach*, that signifies an armor that protects you. Goddess Chandraghanta is loaded with this ultimate armor, which represents spiritual practices that free us from the desires that cause us

## ABOUT AGNI—
## THE FIRE OF TRANSFORMATION

According to Ayurveda, having a healthy digestive fire (known as *agni* in Sanskrit) gives you courage, confidence, and fearlessness to face the challenges of your life from a place of spiritual power. Having a healthy agni gives you joy, cheerfulness, mental clarity, purity, comprehension, consistency, and compassion. Digestion is the essence of having strong immunity, reasoning, and decision-making capacity per Ayurveda. It is responsible for giving you glowing skin, longevity, and physical and emotional strength.

so much suffering and so many feelings of incompleteness. For example, it is the desire for love from others that often keeps us stuck in cycles of trauma and pain. It is the desire to feel full and satisfy our senses that causes us to harm our own bodies through overeating and eating foods that are detrimental to us.

One fascinating part of day 3 is the way in which the actual and metaphorical idea of digestion plays a key role in the process of transformation. In Ayurveda, digestion is understood to be like a fire. When your fire is low, you can't digest food properly. The food you've eaten, in this case, sits in your stomach, raw and unprocessed. Our emotions and life experiences work the same way. When you do not do the work it takes to process, digest, and assimilate your emotions into fuel and "nutrients" you can integrate into your being, they become toxic and remain in your body and mind for a long time. The toxicity of unprocessed food, as well as challenging emotions and life experiences, is the root cause of many diseases according to Ayurveda (and this is being corroborated by modern science as well).

This is why I was only able to fully, and irreversibly, heal myself from eating disorders by understanding their relationship to the childhood trauma I experienced and eventually "digesting" that experience. I tried for many years to avoid facing the pain of this early trauma, the memories of which I could not suppress, no matter how hard I tried to "suck it all up." I finally realized that entering the fire of transformation means being willing to face your own shadow (the parts of you that you've disowned), look straight at what scares you the most, and see and recognize all the kinds of masks you might have worn as defense mechanisms against being vulnerable and real.

## Knowing CHANDRAGHANTA

In Durga's first incarnation as Shailputri, she immolated herself out of love for Lord Shiva. In her second incarnation, she performed brahma-

charya in order to remarry Shiva as Brahmacharini. Now, in Durga's third incarnation, Chandraghanta, the story comes full circle. Lord Shiva has become detached from worldly affairs and has retired into the mountains in deep meditation, isolation, and penance after losing Shailputri.

Seeing Brahmacharini's resolve to marry him again in her new birth, Shiva agrees, but on the day of their marriage, he appears with ashes of the dead smeared on his body, with snakes around his neck, and without bothering to comb his matted, unsightly hair. Even worse, his gruesome marriage procession includes ghosts, goblins, ghouls, naked ascetics, and sages. Brahmacharini's mother and other relatives faint from terror.

In that moment, Durga transforms from Brahmacharini to Chandraghanta, a fierce avatar of Durga with three eyes and ten hands. She rides a lion and carries a weapon in each of her hands. She is ready for war—a holy war, that is. She has a fiery, golden, sun-colored complexion. Her body becomes celestial, full of hot fire. She radiates so much light, in fact, that her mere appearance requires a lot of visual energy to take in!

Chandraghanta is not angry; she is powerful beyond measure and makes no excuses for her fierce stance when Shiva's strange behaviors terrify her mother and family members. She persuades him to transform himself into a handsome prince, with a much nobler marriage procession. Shiva then returns as Prince Charming, bedecked in jewels instead of ashes.

As in chapter 2, though this is the story of a man and a woman, it is not meant to be understood literally. Instead, the story of Shiva and Chandraghanta can be taken as the story of the ongoing struggle to expose and to unite with our true Self. This unexpected marriage story highlights how we all must find the power and strength within to take a stand for what we believe is right, which benefits others and ourselves, and ultimately allows for genuine change and connection.

It is certainly not easy to be fierce and compassionate at the same time. That is why Goddess Chandraghanta is armed with so many weapons, which are symbolic of destroying inner demons. When we acknowledge our emotions fully (by feeling them however we can) and learn to transmute them (rather than getting overwhelmed by them), we become empowered to fight outer battles by being both fiercely loving and strong. This is because the Self in us is the same as the Self in any other

## TRANSFORMATION & THE THIRD CHAKRA

The power of transformation dwells in your third chakra (also called the solar plexus), which is located in your navel area, your sacred core. This is the place where you connect with your personal power, assert yourself when necessary, and find your place in the world. The third (solar plexus) chakra is fueled by the fire element and the sense of sight. By balancing your third chakra, you can achieve the incredible health, balance, and power that come from proper digestion of your food, information, emotions, and life experiences.

Chandraghanta is loaded with weaponry, which is appropriate considering the intensity of the battles necessary to fight both inner and outer demons that block you from your true power. On the spiritual journey, there are many lessons that teach us the power and importance of love, compassion, gentleness, and forgiveness. This is very important, and Goddess Chandraghanta in your third chakra, with all her weapons, reminds us of the necessity to also have healthy boundaries, and to practice bravery when we go through the fire of transformation to purify the ego, so it is healthy but not excessive. This ensures your energy can start to rise into the higher chakras that follow.

being. Fighting for the greatest good of all (without ever forgetting our own needs) is what it means to be a true spiritual warrior. When we can wage war with our own anger, resolve it for ourselves, and then engage in battles in which we recognize the spiritual oneness we all share, we are more likely to emerge from such conflicts victorious. We will know how to set appropriate boundaries when needed, but it all comes from a place of divine, fierce love.

## Taking Inventory

When it comes to transformation, it helps to first check in with yourself to know whether you are operating from your ego's power or from the power of your soul.

Determining which power you resonate with more in each category below will also help you identify which areas you can specifically work on to align yourself more with the freedom and power of your soul and to bring about the deepest, most lasting wellness.

| | STRONGLY AGREE | AGREE | NEITHER AGREE NOR DISAGREE | DISAGREE | STRONGLY DISAGREE |
|---|---|---|---|---|---|
| I draw my power from within. | 1 | 2 | 3 | 4 | 5 |
| I can stand my ground with inner knowledge of my own power when insulted. | 1 | 2 | 3 | 4 | 5 |
| I feel powerful whether or not others approve of my actions. | 1 | 2 | 3 | 4 | 5 |
| If I need to correct others' behaviors and mistakes, I can do so from a place of compassion and understanding that we are all in process. | 1 | 2 | 3 | 4 | 5 |

| | STRONGLY AGREE | AGREE | NEITHER AGREE NOR DISAGREE | DISAGREE | STRONGLY DISAGREE |
|---|---|---|---|---|---|
| I accommodate my own learning curve and mistakes with a sense of dignity. | 1 | 2 | 3 | 4 | 5 |
| I am gentle with myself when I make mistakes. | 1 | 2 | 3 | 4 | 5 |
| I have healthy boundaries. | 1 | 2 | 3 | 4 | 5 |
| I speak up in the face of injustice. | 1 | 2 | 3 | 4 | 5 |
| I feel connected to the present moment. | 1 | 2 | 3 | 4 | 5 |
| I can practice letting go and relaxing in the face of uncertainty. | 1 | 2 | 3 | 4 | 5 |
| I trust in a universal intelligence and presence. | 1 | 2 | 3 | 4 | 5 |
| I ask for help when I need to make changes in my life. | 1 | 2 | 3 | 4 | 5 |
| I do not have to do everything perfectly. | 1 | 2 | 3 | 4 | 5 |
| I can be truthful about my own needs (physical and emotional) and limitations. | 1 | 2 | 3 | 4 | 5 |
| I can be vulnerable with others. | 1 | 2 | 3 | 4 | 5 |
| I can validate my own actions to feel powerful and worthy. | 1 | 2 | 3 | 4 | 5 |

If you scored anywhere from 16 to 36 points, your soul power is strong.

If you scored between 37 and 59 points, you know what it means to be in touch with your soul power, and you can use your strength to keep choosing soul power over ego power.

If you scored between 60 and 80 points, your ego may be running the show, but have no fear, as awareness is the first step of transformation.

# Igniting the Fire of Transformation

Oftentimes, we know there are things that we wish to change, but we are unable to implement the steps it takes to invite lasting transformation of different kinds (big or small) in our lives. Just as our strong emotions lead us toward what it is we wish to transform in the first place, we can learn to trust and work with these emotions to ignite the kind of lasting transformation we seek in our lives.

*Invite your emotions, especially anger and fear, to rise to the surface of your awareness.*

If you don't feel anger when your boundaries have been violated, you won't be able to take the actions you need to take. This is especially relevant in cases of trauma that occur in childhood. When we experience trauma as children, we often blame ourselves for it. We also learn that to survive, we must become caretakers for our out-of-control adults, and in the process, we learn to deny our feelings and needs. In my own case, this process of awakening began when I started studying in California. During the first nine months, I consciously invited my anger to come to the surface as the first step to healing my own experiences of childhood trauma. I needed to feel my anger to find the power to transform my life.

Along with anger, you must come face-to-face, in many ways, with fear when igniting the fire of transformation. In Yoga psychology, one of the root causes of suffering is the fear of death, *abhinivesha* in Sanskrit. In fact, Vedic spiritual tradition teaches that all fear is rooted in the fear of death. Reincarnation is also a core belief of the Vedic spiritual tradition. As human beings, we are programmed, by our very nature, to fear death and resist change, but according to ancient wisdom traditions, all change involves a death of the old to make way for the birth of the new.

The more we can understand, as the Bhagavad Gita teaches, that death is nothing but the changing of clothes, from one "bodysuit" to another in the form of reincarnation, the less we need to fear death. And the less we fear death, the less we need to fear anything else in life.

## Understand where your emotions come from.

Make a list of what upsets you. Every point on this list is important because you are important. Express your emotions to yourself by capturing them on paper.

In my own case, the story of Shailputri standing up to her father and immolating herself in the sacrificial fire, and then the one of Chandraghanta standing up for herself while being armed with weapons, courage, and bravery beyond belief made a deep impression upon me.

I couldn't help but experience these stories viscerally as I had been afraid of my parents, especially my dad, for my whole life. My dad was very strict and made many "family rules" that we all were supposed to follow. If I dared disobey, intentionally or unintentionally, my dad, as many parents do to discipline their children, hit me or punished me by sending me downstairs to the dark basement.

One family rule that was hard for me was always eating everything on my plate. I have many memories of my mom making eggplant, which I did not want to eat because it did not agree with my body (something I was amazed to have confirmed by personalized Ayurvedic dietary guidance years later). I prayed every night that my mom would make anything but eggplant, so I wouldn't be punished and force-fed food that my body rejected.

Though the punishments never left a physical scar, the sheer terror of those times was not something I could easily shake off. It stayed in my body and manifested as eating disorders as I got older. Though I did not hurt anyone else, I took the blame for what had happened and punished myself by internalizing punishing behaviors toward myself, and thereby unconsciously perpetuated the cycle of trauma from my earlier years.

I used to not communicate very much with my parents, or would do so reluctantly, out of the deep-seated fear of those early memories replaying themselves. About nine months after I began studying Ayurveda, and the first time I celebrated Navratri during that period of study, I resolved to confront my parents on the night when we celebrated Goddess Chandraghanta. Before I could do that, though, I first had to tell them how I had been studying Ayurveda. I knew they would be angry that I had left my career in business, so I had kept it a secret because I still felt afraid of my father.

## Accept the situation as it is.

Acceptance is a powerful spiritual step toward growth and evolution. None of us were born perfect. We may not always behave properly in all situations. Not everything will be in our control. Despite that, we must learn to accept ourselves, others, and every situation in our lives, including those we wish to transform, as a prerequisite to making change.

Many times, it feels as if it might be easier to simply sweep deeper issues under the rug and avoid dealing with them. Denial is a very common coping strategy when there is pain, but it perpetuates repetition of negative behaviors that we may wish to transform. I myself tried to deny my pain for many years by pretending to be fine and faking a smile when I really wanted to cry. A big cause of anorexia nervosa, according to Ayurveda, is suppression of tears, which happens when we push against simply accepting what is.

Discernment of what we can and cannot control is an important step in empowering us to detach from what happened to us in the past (which we cannot control) and thereby accept it. Without discernment, then detachment, and eventually acceptance, we tend to blindly repeat negative patterns; however, when we look toward the future with acceptance of the past, we are our own master.

Writing our own destiny to manifest in the future is in our own hands. When you apply effort to change your current karma, the effect you produce in your life can eventually and irreversibly improve the course of your karmic destiny. When you take on the practice of waking up early, for example, after many years of sleeping in, you have to first accept how you feel when waking up late. Once you continuously awaken early over a period of time (provided you also go to sleep early), your mind will start to feel clearer and calmer, and you will have more energy, provided you keep up this new practice as a dedicated habit.

### Forgive the person(s) who upset you (and forgive yourself for allowing boundaries to be crossed or for doing something you regret).

Forgiveness does not mean condoning wrong actions. It simply means opening our hearts to compassion and love for us all as we make our journeys through our human bodies and lives and fumble and forget who we really are and do ignorant things as a result along the way. Forgiveness cannot be forced. Just as we invite our emotions to come to the surface, we have to invite forgiveness, set an intention within to forgive, and simply allow it to blossom in its own time once we have deeply accepted situations for what they are. We also have to forgive ourselves for all the times we have hurt ourselves by accepting harmful treatment from others and for harming ourselves, even in small ways, like when we choose to eat burgers instead of fruits, even though the burgers are not helping us.

I remember receiving a fortune cookie at a Chinese restaurant amidst a horrible fight between my dad and me. The fortune said, "One who hurts another hurts oneself the most." I remember how deeply that aphorism resonated with me and opened my heart, even in the heat of the argument we were having.

### Find the lesson you learned from the situation as a way to arrive at greater resolve within yourself.

Your learning could be as simple as confirming from your experience of sleeping late why it is important to wake up earlier. Your resolve may be to overcome your own resistance to going to sleep early so that you can awaken early each morning and have more time and energy to complete your tasks for the day ahead. Usually, it's less about what you resist doing than *why* you resist doing something that is most healing. It helps to ask yourself: Is there a part of me that resists doing this? Why? And can I bring love to this younger part of myself?

On my own journey, I arrived at the lesson of breaking the cycle of trauma within my own family through the power of love, compassion, and forgiveness. My father, having left India to create a better life for his family in the West, focused greatly on providing for us financially. Because I was always comfortable financially as a result of his sacrifices, I had the luxury of time to dig deep into spirituality. In the process of doing so, I resolved to never repeat this cycle again, by connecting with the power of the Truth, to set us all free. Because I am not punishing toward others, but had a pattern of internalizing punishments toward myself, I resolved to let that old behavior die by deeply connecting with the eternal power of my own soul. I knew I also needed to do this as a way to ensure that I would not myself one day unconsciously repeat my dad's mistakes and traumatize my own future children, as it is so easy to simply blindly repeat what others have done to us otherwise.

I wrote in my journal on the night dedicated to Chandraghanta during my first inward celebration of Navratri:

> My sankalpa [resolved intention] today is to die to my previous forms, to be born again as my true nature. To allow my eternal, internal sun [soul] to destroy the outer forms I've been forced to assume, to truly free myself from the prison of my own mind. To burn through falsehood and illusion to identify fully with the strength of my soul, which was never born and will never die.

> To allow my words to come from a space of unconditional love: for myself and for others, who are really my Self. Specifically, to tell my parents about my resolve to be committed to studying and living by Ayurveda, that I have moved out of respect for myself to live in a peaceful environment, am quitting my job to be able to study Ayurveda, and am moving forward on my business plan. If it doesn't work, I will start applying for other jobs as backup to give me enough money for rent, tuition, and time to be committed to study. I will sell my car if needed and live in a lesser place, as I don't care for money and status; my aim is and always has been to be of service: to live in peace and be able to spread that peace to others by my example.

Knowing and understanding that the soul is eternal gives us unparalleled power in the face of fear when we try to overcome obstacles in our lives and free ourselves from karmic cycles. Transformation necessitates a death of the old ways, which can feel terrifying and cause us to remain attached to our pain, suffering, and "victim story." When we truly learn and develop faith in who we really are, as embodied eternal souls, we can rid ourselves of the attachments we have to any kind of victimhood and rise above feelings of oppression.

One of the keys to setting these intentions is to focus, as hard as it may be, on what you stand to gain. In my case, the answer was straightforward: freedom. I wrote:

> My core need is freedom, and I'm willing to sacrifice some of my comforts to have this.

### Take action to implement your resolve.

It may take many cycles through day 3 to be ready to act. In my own case, it took nine months before I told my parents the truth about my plans for the future.

After listening to them yell about my decision (all while remembering that Goddess Chandraghanta lives within me), I finally spoke up and told my father how I saw the situation. I explained that I felt our family was caught in a cycle of damaging behaviors and that when we experienced dark things, we either inflicted the pain on others or we inflicted it upon ourselves. I calmly but assertively said that he had passed on what he had suffered from my grandfather to my mom, sister, and me. I had internalized it through my eating disorders to the point that I no longer wanted to live. I was making different choices for myself because Ayurveda had given me a second chance at life.

Suddenly my dad's anger and rage turned to tears and sorrow. There had been only a handful of times in my life up until then when I had seen him break down. He explained how he really didn't know any better because that's how his father raised him. I told him I understood and how I intended to break the cycle now, forever.

A couple of weeks later during Diwali, a sacred Vedic festival during which we celebrate Goddess Lakshmi, my dad visited me in California, and we attended an Ayurveda class together. The next day, I led him in Sandhya Vandanam, the same ancient cleansing ritual I mentioned in chapter 2, which is also used to symbolically let go of negative karmic patterns from your parents so you can ultimately carve out your own karmic destiny. *Sandhya* itself means "transition" and *vandanam* means "thanksgiving." It was truly a transition marked by gratitude. In that way, we rid ourselves of the past and were able to move forward into the future with a transformed parent-child relationship.

I feel so grateful that my dad was willing to undergo the fire of transformation with me, and for how our relationship has transformed into an unexpected friendship for which I feel eternally grateful. To heal my trauma of mealtimes as times of terror and punishment, I initiated a practice of having everyone in my family express their gratitude for each other before holiday meals. Year after year, when my dad's turn comes around, he reminds us that life is a learning curve, that we must learn something new every day, and that we always learn more from our mistakes than our successes. He cries every time he shares. He apologizes for his mistakes and reassures me that I need not fear sharing with him anymore as he trusts my judgment.

I truly admire and look up to my dad for how he has accepted his own learning curve and mistakes with a sense of dignity and humility. His unconditional support of my power as a woman (after testing my resolve) is what inspires me to forge new transformational pathways for women's empowerment today. And seeing the way my dad has grown and softened over the years, and become one of the greatest, most loyal supporters of my spiritual path, has reinforced for me the power of transformation.

# The Path Forward: Practices for Transformation

PRACTICE: *Roar away your fears in Lion's Pose.*

Fear is a major obstacle to practicing detachment. The fear of letting go can cause you to stay trapped in limiting situations and harmful relationships. It causes you to lose your power and connection with your true spiritual essence.

Goddess Chandraghanta rides a lion. When you feel afraid, you can call upon this goddess and her majestic lion as friends who symbolize bravery in the face of the greatest fear. We have to come face-to-face with our fears to practice letting go of all that we are not in order to embrace the spiritual power that exists at the core of our being, in the third chakra.

Ancient sages from every tradition have revealed the power of observing nature closely. From their observations of the natural world, they have gifted humanity with yogic poses that help us to embody the spirit and essence of nature.

When you approach Lion's Pose by feeling yourself becoming as powerful and strong as a lion, it empowers you to become just that. It helps so much, therefore, to look up videos of lions roaring. And then to envision yourself roaring just like the lion, and that you are roaring directly at whatever it is that scares you the most, whether that be fear of a loss of a person or situation, fear of a bully, or even fear of expressing your truth.

You have to "name it to tame it," as many modern psychologists say. This yogic pose provides an opportunity to do so. Once you have done this, you can then practice the pose with the full power it gives you to start to roar your fears away, with the support of Goddess Chandraghanta, who you can ask for courage in your heart.

Instructions for practice:

1. Sit on your knees and spread them apart. Place your hands on the ground in front of you and turn your arms so your elbows come toward your body and your fingers also point toward your body. Tuck your hands under your thighs.

2. Lean forward like a lion about to pounce. Press the weight of your body onto your arms, with your elbows pressing against your abdomen.

3. Inhale deeply through your nose. Then open your mouth, extend your tongue, open your eyes wide, and exhale by making a noise that sounds like a lion's roar.

4. Repeat three to five times, pausing between each roar to gently massage your throat.

**PRACTICE:** *Do something (positive) that scares you.*

Eleanor Roosevelt is often quoted as saying, "You must do the thing you think you cannot do." I find this to be so very true. The more I do things that scare me, the closer I feel to my true Self. When we face our fears, our fears vanish. And all we are left with is our divine essence.

It requires reflection to ascertain exactly what you should do. In my life, teaching, writing, healing and caring for others, and organizing and bringing people together for a common cause come easily. Being visible in public, being on camera, expressing my deeper truth, facing my past, and handling intimate relationships were initially extremely challeng-ing for me, and remain that way at times. Approaching each thing that brings up fear and resistance within me by remembering that Goddess Chandraghanta lives in my heart empowers me to do what I feel I ought to do, which, for me, are always actions in service of health and spiritual-ity for all.

If you are a teacher, for example, then you ought to teach. Not for ego gratification. And not even to help or uplift another (though that would be an unselfish thing to do). The goal is to make your action so pure that it can free you from the bondage of desire and lead you to connection with your true Self. So teach (or do whatever you are capable of) for its own sake, without attachment to results. The purest actions are those that are free from desire and, as a result, bring you closer to your spiritual es-sence; these actions may scare you, but you take them because you feel it is your duty to perform them for the higher good of all.

**PRACTICE:** *Light a lamp with the intention of burning away an obstacle you face.*

While immersed in my nine-year solo spiritual pilgrimage to know my own Self, I used to light a lamp every morning. Doing so was a way to connect with the power of my inner light, to be able to face the dark forces that beset us all at times.

The light of the lamp in the ancient Vedic spiritual tradition represents our attempts to find light amidst the darkness, because of who we are as spiritual beings, with all the power imaginable within ourselves. We just forget who we are, and hence lose our power. The whole purpose of the spiritual journey, therefore, is to constantly remember your soul power.

Lighting a lamp or candle is one of many ways to ignite this deepest memory of your true identity as a soul (not the body, mind, or intellect). As you ignite this memory, resistance to obstacles is vanquished. When you pair the physical practice of lighting a lamp with owning the inner intention of overcoming obstacles you face, it empowers you to connect with the power of Goddess Chandraghanta within you. It helps when doing this practice to affirm that "the light and fire of Goddess Chandraghanta lives inside me as the power of a thousand radiant suns."

## PRACTICE: *Eat warm, cooked foods.*

In Ayurveda, the key to transformation in your third chakra is in digesting your food, which helps you digest the information you take in as well as your emotions and life experiences. When you eat warm, cooked foods, you can do so by setting an intention to offer the food you eat to ignite the power of Goddess Chandraghanta within you.

The heat of the fire from the cooking process is purifying. Eating warm, cooked foods supports the transformation of what you eat into nutrients your body can use for immunity and strength. It's like when you wash the dishes. Warm water clears the dirt from the dishes a lot more easily than when you try to clean them with cold water. Your body works similarly. Warm substances cleanse toxins from your system, whereas colder substances allow them to fester and even multiply. When you feed your body warm substances, your digestive fire is kindled, whereas cold substances extinguish it.

So many of my students report what a world of difference simply shifting from cold, raw foods to warm, cooked foods makes in terms of digestion. This one simple shift can help turn around chronic constipation and clear up other health issues, as a healthy, balanced digestion is considered key to overall health at all levels.

**PRACTICE:** *Incorporate digestion-promoting spices into your food.*

You can evoke the power of transformation with spices. Most Ayurvedic spices have a lot of the fire element, connected with Goddess Chandraghanta in your third chakra.

One of these spices is black pepper. The Sanskrit name for black pepper is *maricha*, one of the names for the sun, the greatest source of fire on earth. Black pepper imparts an intense, burning heat and fire so you can better digest your food (don't use it if you suffer from heartburn, acid reflux, or other heat-related issues). Cumin seeds are like a matchstick to ignite your digestion but are mild enough that they will not burn your body. Fennel seeds are a sweeter digestion-promoting and heartburn-relieving spice. Coriander seeds are a unique spice that boosts your digestive fire while simultaneously removing heat from your body.

You can incorporate any of these spices into your favorite savory cooking (ideally in ghee, or clarified butter, which is an immunity- and digestion-boosting cooking medium). Even if you don't cook, adding ¼ teaspoon of any or all of these spices (based on your personal needs) to your food will benefit your digestion.

**PRACTICE:** *Sit in Thunderbolt Pose after eating to promote digestion of your food, emotions, and life experiences.*

Thunderbolt Pose is named after the Vedic god Indra's lightning bolt, a weapon used to bring about goodness and restore confidence in the face of darkness. You can connect with this powerful energy within yourself after each meal. I love how this one yogic posture connects the best of your physical manifestation (your third chakra, where you create health through your ability to digest) with your highest consciousness (your higher chakras).

Goddess Chandraghanta in your third chakra gives you the power to devour all forms of foods and diseases, as well as grief and resistances, which she burns away. She also bestows you with healthy digestive fire, when you remember her in the form of your own digestion and practices that bring about healthy digestion.

To practice Thunderbolt Pose, sit up straight after you finish eating, with your eyes closed, for several minutes. Visualize a thunderbolt full of immunity, vitality, strength, and the power to digest everything in your life. This streak of energy connects the base of your spine to the top of your head. Every time you do this pose, imagine digesting and transforming everything that has entered your body into something positive.

## PRACTICE: *Give yourself permission.*

This is one of the most powerful practices that has empowered me to break free from my own personal attachments. "I give myself permission" is a mantra that speaks to my deepest subconscious being and helps me overcome the power games others have played with me over the years.

To give yourself permission, you must first embrace the power of self-approval. Though I always had a brave and bold disposition like Goddess Chandraghanta, when I was younger, I was extremely sensitive to disapproval.

I remember talking with my mom as a teenager. She looked into my eyes and got scared when she saw a lioness in me. She didn't like it, and that hurt me. I started hiding my power from that day on, so as not to lose her love and the love of others.

To reclaim my power, I first had to give myself permission to own my power. It's scary at first, but the intention of giving myself permission helps me define life on my own terms, apart from the expectations and wishes that people like my parents, other well-meaning relatives, and even friends place on me.

Giving myself permission happens most effectively for me when I write down my intentions for what I specifically want to give myself permission to do or feel. For example, I had to give myself permission to feel angry about the trauma I experienced in childhood, which led to even more experiences of trauma in my early adult life. Anger in women is not looked kindly upon, so it was not something I had connected with in myself before that.

Giving yourself permission can mean carving out a safe container of space for yourself to feel long-hidden emotions. It can mean giving yourself permission to embark upon a new wellness routine that may rock the boat with your family but that you know will ultimately lead to healing. Giving yourself permission may mean launching your own business or podcast, something you never allowed yourself to do for whatever reason.

Before undertaking this new activity, write the mantra for yourself: "I give myself permission to ___" and then fill in the blank. The first step is always the hardest part of making changes, and the start of all great things in your life begins with giving yourself permission.

## PRACTICE: *Stand up for yourself.*

This is, by far, one of the best things you can do when you need to take back your personal power in the face of adversity. Goddess Chandraghanta is the perfect role model when it comes to standing up for yourself. When she bellows, demons run to take cover, but she is not angry; she is strong and makes no excuses about being so.

Chandraghanta teaches us when we must stand behind a cause and when it is time to go to war and win the battle for *dharma*, the greatest good of all. A practical example of this is when one parent abuses another and the children in the family. It is necessary for the abused spouse to take a stand for the good of the whole family.

Lao-tzu once said, "The best fighter is never angry." Healthy anger is necessary to feel and experience fully, to register when your boundaries have been violated. It comes as an internal warning that helps you find the courage to fight back. But before actually standing up for yourself, it really helps to work out your anger by releasing it. You can do this through writing, punching a punching bag, martial arts (my personal favorite way to channel anger in a healthy, constructive way), or talking with someone you trust. Give this process time. It should involve the release of tears as well. Grief lives underneath anger, so you must let go of grief to free yourself from attachment, which keeps you powerless.

Once you have processed anger like this, you will be prepared to stand up for yourself by coming from an inner space of compassion for yourself and the other person. This is important, as anyone who has harmed you does so because they feel hurt themselves. When you reach a space of being able to feel compassion for the other person (or people), your compassion empowers you to act in a powerful way, for the greatest good, free from the negative grip of anger. This is what it means to become a true spiritual warrior like Goddess Chandraghanta.

PRACTICE: *Repeat the mantra "I am a powerful being."*

Throughout my life, I have encountered people who did not like my power and did all they could to take it away from me. When I was younger, and not knowledgeable about spirituality, I used to give away my power to try to get emotional security by making others feel comfortable. Meanwhile, a part of me steadily died inside.

My search for spirituality was very much a quest to reclaim my power even though it took many years and much patience to achieve this goal.

Power, after all, is spiritual. It is not about what office, position, or status you possess. It is not about money or looks or book knowledge or any outer achievements.

The Bhagavad Gita, the bible of the Yoga tradition and one of the world's greatest spiritual textbooks for how to live in a peaceful and empowered way, says regarding the power of the soul:

*Weapons cannot cleave it.*

*Fire cannot burn it.*

*Water cannot wet it.*

*Wind cannot dry it.*

There is a Sanskrit term, *avinashi*, meaning "indestructible." When I went through a long, dark tunnel of people trying their best to grab my power, I constantly reminded myself that I am avinashi. I am a powerful being because I am, first and foremost, a spiritual being. As a result of this constant reminder, I got through to the end of that tunnel, transformed, and restarted my life on my own terms.

## "I am a powerful being because I am a spiritual being."

It seems deceptively simple, but the empowerment that comes when you simply remember this one mantra, "I am a powerful being because I am a spiritual being," is incredible. You are already a powerful being. It's simply a matter of remembering your power. By consciously repeating this mantra in your mind, especially in the face of obstacles, challenges, and bullies of different kinds, you will experience a dramatic increase in your own power and light in the face of darkness.

# Chapter 4

# The Art
# of Loving Your
# True Self

*You must lift yourself, by yourself. Do not lower yourself. Your self alone is your friend. Your self alone is your enemy.*

—BHAGAVAD GITA, chapter 6, verse 5

## Cultivating Love

What is love? It's a question human beings have been asking for millennia across all cultures and traditions. When you hear the word *love*, your thoughts might jump immediately to romantic love. Or perhaps you imagine your family, a beloved friend, or even a pet. Certainly, love *is* all of these things, but within the Vedic spiritual tradition, love is so much more than the love we extend to and receive from others. It means realizing your oneness with all living beings. When you truly feel at one with the whole world, this is love. It is a sovereign state of being that includes all.

Unfortunately, we human beings often confuse love and attachment. There is, however, an important distinction between the two that we must discern regularly for the sake of our own emotional sovereignty and for the health of all our relationships. Swami Parthasarathy shares beautiful mathematical equations to express the difference between love and attachment:

$$\text{Love} + \text{Selfishness} = \text{Attachment}$$
$$\text{Attachment} - \text{Selfishness} = \text{True Love}$$

Our own desires (for approval, affection, recognition, and validation from others) pollute our ability to truly love others as our own Self. When we do things for other people (in relationships, work, and situations like posting on social media) with a desire for something in return, we operate out of attachment. Our attachments are what stand in the way of experiencing true love.

As Swami Rama Tirtha once revealed: "The way to gain anything is to lose it." As paradoxical as it may sound, it is true. We must give up the lower (attachments to our desires) to gain the higher (love, which respects our own sovereignty as well as that of others).

The more beings we seek to benefit with our actions, the purer our hearts become, and the more joyful and loving we feel. This emotional state automatically renders our actions more powerful and tends to more easily attract greater outer success.

Though I enjoy every day of the cycle, I particularly appreciate day 4 for its heart-opening qualities. Sometimes I spend this day processing heartbreak, but more often, it's a day of infusing my relationships and work with happiness, laughter, and joy that comes from within.

I especially appreciate day 4 because of my own hard-won experience. On this path, I have seen how self-love is the ultimate love because it is only when we love ourselves that we can love others. That sentiment may be something you have heard before, but this day, this week, this month is a chance to consider what it really means to love your true Self.

My path to loving myself came most powerfully through the dissolution of my relationship with a friend whom I greatly trusted and loved. When we had a disagreement, as all friends do, I was shocked to be on the receiving end of her betrayal and rage. Because of the Navratri practice (specifically, because of constantly remembering that I am a powerful being and touching my heart and affirming "I love myself unconditionally"), I was able to heal the relationship before realizing that letting go of the friendship was the best way to honor my own true Self and that of my friend.

In this chapter, I'll introduce you to Kushmanda, the fourth avatar of Durga. Together, we'll explore how to take inventory of your values, needs, and feelings, and how to discern between love and attachment in your work and relationships. Then I will guide you through steps you can take to make space for true love to shine forth in all that you do, so you can actually *become* love itself.

## Knowing KUSHMANDA

Goddess Kushmanda is called the Smiling Goddess, and the meaning of her name is "little cosmic egg." After taking on the ferociously loving form of Chandraghanta, Durga transforms herself into Kushmanda, the mother of the entire universe.

Before the universe came into being, when darkness ruled, Kushmanda produced a little cosmic egg with her beautiful smile. This served to fill the universe with the radiant light of the sun. Kushmanda dwells in the land of the sun and gives energy to all beings, whom she created from her vast being. She is so powerful and loving that she even gives guidance to the Sun God!

After creating the universe, Mother Kushmanda created beings to reside in her divine cosmic creation. The first three were Goddesses Kali, Lakshmi,

and Saraswati, who represent the powers of purification, abundance, and wisdom. Kushmanda, as the power of all creation in the universe, made it so that these three powerful goddesses gave birth to three powerful male gods. She matched each god with a different goddess. From there, the male gods were imbued with the seed of creation of new living beings.

Kushmanda is the cosmic egg of all creation on earth. She also lives in our hearts. The fact that she is smiling reminds us that we too are our most creative when we are smiling and feeling positive, courageous (a quality of the heart), and strong. The fact that this goddess, like Chandraghanta, rides a lion shows that the power of love is just as potent as the fire of transformation. It reminds us that the ability to love comes from inner strength. When we feel clouded by fear, anger, and grief, it can be difficult to imagine one day having the strength to love again. But Kushmanda is here to remind us that, no matter how brokenhearted we may feel at times, the power of love lives within us, and we can tap into it and become our creative best at any time.

Compassion and love are not weaknesses. They are qualities that only truly powerful people can feel and express. After we've stood up for ourselves, even to our significant other (as Chandraghanta did), we are asked to open our hearts to the healing power of love. To truly love others, even those who have hurt us, we have to, first and foremost, love ourselves. When we remember that this power to love is a gift that we can best give others by first giving it to ourselves, we will feel our strongest and most inspired from within. This will help us overcome the common trap of seeking love in all the wrong places, like from abusive partners, addictive behaviors, and escapism into work, food, or other sources of achievement or satisfaction. We do all these things when we avoid feeling pain in our hearts. But to heal, we have to feel. Once we have opened ourselves to feeling our pain (in whatever way feels natural to us), Goddess Kushmanda is there in our hearts to remind us that all that is left is love.

> ## To heal, we have to feel.

It is impossible to choose a favorite goddess, as they are all so inspiring and powerful for their unique purposes, but if I had to choose one, it would be Kushmanda. Feeling her in my heart has helped me heal so many deep wounds in my life and given me the strength to start anew after experiences of great loss. Whenever I remember Kushmanda, I smile to myself and remember that the spiritual journey is not to be

## LOVE & THE FOURTH CHAKRA

The power of love is connected with your fourth chakra (called the heart chakra). It is located in your heart area. This is where your energy starts moving into the higher realms of awareness, beyond your ego, and closer to your higher Self. The heart chakra is like a breath of fresh air. It is associated with the air element and the sense of touch. Cultivating the power of love by balancing the fourth chakra brings you the gift of self-love, which is a necessary foundation to love all others and manifest abundance in your work.

Kushmanda is depicted as laughing. After going through the journey of purification of the ego in the previous three chakras, we are now reminded to not take ourselves too seriously on our spiritual journey! Kushmanda's laughter reminds us that when we are laughing (not stressing) is when we are the most creative. Opening your heart chakra leads to experiencing self-love, the kind of love that gives you fulfillment in life.

taken too seriously. When I can relax, I am able to create and share love from a place where I am not seeking anything in return.

## Taking Inventory

Even just thinking about love in your life can bring on feelings of deep joy but also of deep sorrow. Unfortunately, it will be impossible to truly make the changes you seek without honestly assessing the relationships you have with others, with your work, and most important, with yourself. Because it's so easy to lose ourselves in work, relationships, and things like social media, we need to make a concerted effort to define our values as our anchor. It is also necessary to spend time getting in touch with your own feelings and needs and to look non-judgmentally at where the invisible, yet potent, grip of attachment has crept up in your life.

When we start to live in alignment with our values, we not only extend love to others, but we actually become love. And when we become love, we automatically feel full from within ourselves. We no longer need to beg for love and approval from others; we can instead take responsibility for our own needs and feelings, to ensure we are able to continue to be embodiments of pure love.

As you begin the process of taking inventory (and it will be a process that may take a few or many cycles through day 4 with Goddess Kushmanda), you can first ask yourself what your values are and what is most important to you. From there, you can also pose these questions:

- How do I truly feel right now? (Sometimes I have to ask myself this question over and over again to arrive at my reality, as my feelings have often been labeled by others as unacceptable.) How do I feel about my relationships? Work? Social media feeds?

- What core needs do I have that I am not willing to compromise for anyone else?

- Do I honor my own feelings and needs when I am with other people?

- If I were alone, would I make different choices than those I make when surrounded by others?

- Which relationships fill me up? Which ones drain me?

- Where have attachments crept up in my life? What keeps me awake at night? Who or what do I have trouble stopping myself from thinking about?

## The Art of Loving Your True Self

The art of loving your true Self is one of the superpowers you experience when you connect with the power of Goddess Kushmanda. I've outlined my own journey to loving myself in this chapter, but I encourage you to modify these steps as needed in order to arrive at a place where you know and love yourself with your whole heart and with the positivity, courage, strength, and joy of the goddess Kushmanda.

### *Make time and space to honor your own needs.*

It is so easy when we prioritize our relationships with others to lose ourselves in the process. Unfortunately, even before we recognize this as a problem, we may feel the emotional upheaval that comes from not honoring our own feelings and needs. That's why it's necessary to come back to yourself and make time to learn about yourself and what you want for your life.

Even after years of study and spiritual practice, I was still so in the habit of prioritizing the needs of others over my own that it took a betrayal by one of my closest friends to open my eyes to how I habitually betrayed myself. I only realized this when I gave myself intentional time to connect with my own needs.

*Observe which emotional needs are being met by your current relationships, work, or other situations (like sharing on social media) where a lot of attachments are present.*

Before we can actually let go of what harms us, we must observe and understand the emotional needs our present situations meet for us. This ensures we can address those needs and prevent ourselves from repeating the same behavioral and relationship patterns in new contexts and with new people.

Dr. Maya Angelou once said, "When people show you who they are, believe them the first time." When my friend and I first disagreed over a work-related situation we were collaborating on, I was forced to observe how I defined my worth by how much I was available to help others. I also tended to give my power away to others in exchange for the emotional security of someone being there for me, even in an unhealthy way. These coping strategies were how I avoided feeling the pain of my own childhood but also how I delayed having to fully step into my own power as a leader (and endure the jealousies and unpleasantness of leadership). In the process, I abandoned myself by not honoring my own needs. I was my own enemy.

*Practice letting go of your attachments from a space of true love.*

The spiritual journey is the most challenging path any of us will ever choose because it involves taking so much responsibility. When we truly understand the law of karma, we become radically responsible beings. We will not blame anyone else for our misfortunes in life but will do whatever we can to dissolve our karma instead of getting angry and acting like victims, which only generates further karma to be resolved in future situations.

Having discovered my unexamined pattern of self-betrayal, I discerned that cutting ties with my false friend would be an act of befriending myself. However, rather than cut ties with her while feeling resentful for her cruel behaviors and feelings toward me, I spent time and energy flowing love toward her, so that by the time I cut my connection with her, she acknowledged feeling loved by me and loving me. Having let go with love leaves me with peace in my heart regarding the fallout.

*Act in alignment with your values, with a spirit of love, joy, play, devotion, and even laughter replacing any attachments to the outcome(s) of your action(s).*

In the Vedas, we learn that love is ultimately expressed through our actions. The Sanskrit word for action, interestingly, is *karma*. What the Vedic spiritual tradition teaches us to practice is karma yoga in terms of our actions. The Bhagavad Gita instructs us on how we can lift ourselves up and be our own friend by being fully present in our actions and simply acting in service of dharma (the greatest good of all) without any attachment to the outcomes of our actions.

After letting go of my friend with love, I committed myself to embodying my full power as a leader by continuously feeling my feelings, loving myself, and discerning and acting upon what I felt I ought to do. It was an incredibly liberating feeling to finally do so.

When you act in accordance with the values you have personally defined as being most important, you become empowered to automatically control your selfish desires and develop your capacity to realize your true Self. You are also supported in becoming abundant, because acting unselfishly for a higher purpose than ourselves feels a lot more empowering than scrambling to fulfill our own baser desires.

I had no idea, in making the choice to let go of my false friend and embrace my own leadership, what the outcome would be. But I definitely felt it was the right thing to do. I felt like a caterpillar that emerged as a butterfly, lighter, happier, and freer as I flew away from drama and restarted

# UNDERSTANDING THE LAW OF KARMA

The law of karma is the most important spiritual law that governs our existence. Nothing happens randomly in this universe. Everything we experience is due to an infinite chain of cause and effect that has led to the present moment. Initially, the law of karma can be a triggering concept because it can feel as if it unfairly puts the blame for abuse onto those who receive it. However, when you truly understand and accept the law of karma, it is actually an extremely empowering force. It can inspire us to know that, just as we are ultimately responsible for everything that happens to us at the deepest level, we are equally capable of rewriting a new life script for ourselves. We can do this by authoring conscious actions in the present that will lead to happier future events, if not immediately, then for sure eventually.

my life on my own terms. I feel grateful I trained myself in practicing karma yoga during periods of difficulty, so that now my work, with much more mature people who possess aligned values, truly feels like play.

## The Path Forward: Practices for Love

PRACTICE: *Touch your heart and affirm, "I love myself unconditionally."*

This is a very simple yet profoundly nurturing practice for healing your heart. It is a way to check in with your emotions and to reassure yourself, no matter what you may be feeling, that you are going to be there

for yourself through your own discomfort. It immediately allows you to soothe and comfort yourself by connecting with your own feelings rather than avoiding or escaping them through unhealthy habits like drinking too much, texting, scrolling through Instagram one too many times, etc.

Your true Self is known in Sanskrit as *santosha*, or "content and cheerful from within." This is different from ordinary contentment or cheerfulness, which both arise from external situations and circumstances. True contentment is present within you regardless of what temporary emotions you may experience in a given moment. When you take a moment (or several moments) to touch your own heart, you give yourself an opportunity to calm anxiety and feel your emotions as a way to heal them and give yourself reassurance that you will be there for you.

## PRACTICE: *Heal your heart with roses.*

Roses are considered a *hrdaya* flower in Ayurveda, meaning they benefit your emotional and physical heart. You can heal your heart from pain, anger, and irritability by simply stopping to smell the roses via rose essential oils or actual roses. Doing so not only uplifts your heart but also helps you feel more grounded. You can also try taking a warm bath with rose petals. This is especially helpful if you feel overworked, overstimulated, or exhausted. Another idea is to spray a rose-infused mist onto your face to help reduce heat in your body.

Roses are edible, and you can make a soothing rose smoothie to take in the heart-healing power of roses too. Here's a recipe you can try:

**INGREDIENTS**

1 large dried fig or 2 medium dried figs (soaked overnight)

2 to 4 organic, pesticide-free rose petals

1 cup almond, oat, rice, or cow's milk

**METHOD**

1. Blend the fig(s) and rose petals to create a beautifully scented paste.
2. Pour the milk into a medium pot. Add the paste and allow it all to boil.
3. Remove the milk from the heat and serve warm.

Roses are excellent for beautifying your skin if it is red, sensitive, aging, or inflamed. You can make a cleanser by mixing ½ tablespoon rose water and ½ tablespoon milk. Then, wash your face with this cleanser and rinse with room-temperature water. You can also exfoliate your skin with 1 teaspoon each of rose water, milk, and rock sugar (ground into a fine powder) mixed with ½ teaspoon honey (if you have hot and oily skin) or ghee (if your skin is dry).

However you choose to benefit from roses, make sure to remember the joyfulness of Goddess Kushmanda dwelling in your heart as you do so.

## PRACTICE: *Love yourself with oil each morning before showering.*

The word for oil in Sanskrit is *sneha*, which also means "to love." Applying warm oil to your skin before taking a shower in the morning, on an empty stomach, is a beautiful way to open your heart chakra and infuse your skin with strength and love. The ancient Ayurvedic texts reveal how oiling your body regularly is a powerful anti-aging practice that relieves exhaustion, nourishes your body, soothes anxiety, and gives you sound sleep, longevity, and glowing skin.

The feeling of oiling your body is like treating yourself with the love and care you would give a baby. In India, women traditionally receive daily oil massages, along with their babies, for forty days or more following birth. The difference it makes to your skin and overall well-being is akin to a piece of shoe leather. Without shining the leather, it gets rough and dry quickly. But when you polish the same leather, it shines. The benefit of this practice goes beyond the barrier of your skin, however, filling you up with your own love, and thereby empowering you to connect with Goddess Kushmanda in your heart.

## Instructions for practice:

You can oil your body with organic sesame oil in cold seasons and organic coconut oil in warm seasons. If it's in between seasons, simply combine both oils.

1. Fill your sink with hot tap water. Warm the oil by placing the bottle in the water for a few minutes.

2. Sit on a towel and, using your fingers, rub the warm oil onto the bottoms of your feet. Then work your way up from your feet to the rest of your body (face is optional). Rub the oil up and down on long bones, and in a circular way when rubbing your joints. Put energy into it. The more vigorously you rub the oil into your skin, the deeper it penetrates, and the more profound its rejuvenating benefits.

3. Give extra love, care, and time to any area that hurts or cracks.

4. Shower with warm water. The heat of the water will allow the oil to travel deeper into your skin.

5. Use moong dal flour as a soap substitute or an aloe vera– or coconut oil–based soap to ensure your skin doesn't get dried out.

## DON'T OIL IF YOU ARE:

- Menstruating
- Constipated or having diarrhea
- Experiencing a cold or cough
- Feverish

- Dealing with wounds or rashes (avoid oiling those areas)
- Experiencing a rainy or cloudy day (environmental moisture makes it hard for your body to absorb oil properly)

**PRACTICE: *Write a letter pouring out your heart to someone you love who disappointed you.***

It is therapeutic to put your emotions on paper. Often, without knowing it, we store unexperienced grief in our hearts, where it blocks us from experiencing love. Therefore, we have to work to release our pain in order to unblock our hearts.

When someone better suited for me appeared in my life a few months after the last time I saw my ex-boyfriend, it was a clear signal from the universe that I needed to fully let go of my ex in my heart. Writing a letter pouring out my sincere, patient love and hope for him to become the great person I always felt he could become really helped relieve my heart. But it was a pain that even a much better match for me could not completely heal.

I had to face the truth of my heart, to feel all my emotions fully, which only writing and then reading the letter over and over to myself (and even aloud to someone I deeply trusted) could really help me with. Once the words reached the page, it felt like they were outside of me. The emotions could be released onto the page, and that left me feeling freer and wiser for the experience of the relationship. I still, of course, cried later when I thought of him, but the fact I had written the letter gave me a feeling of finality, understanding, and resolve that allowed the later emotions to wash over me more easily.

When you write a letter to someone you love who really hurt you, do so with the intention of keeping this expression to yourself. This will help you express everything you need to freely, without fear of consequences.

It takes strength to do this, but it is deeply therapeutic and something you can first call upon Goddess Kushmanda in your heart to support you with. Know that, no matter how painful it is to feel your emotions this way, doing so will help open your heart chakra, so that you can invite in beautiful new relationships and experiences.

PRACTICE: *Listen to soothing music you love.*

Music is the language of the heart. Sometimes when we experience emotional pain, we seek out songs that reflect our sad emotional states, but it also is important and helpful to listen to music that soothes and uplifts. I have created several playlists on Spotify that I love playing to help me feel energized or inspired.

I often like to listen to inspiring music while working on written projects that come from my heart (which I am blessed to have as the majority of my work). Music profoundly affects your emotions, so when you feel sensitive, it is necessary to feed your ears only positive sounds.

PRACTICE: *Eat heart-healing pumpkins and pomegranates.*

There are special foods from Ayurveda designed specifically to heal your heart, physically and emotionally. Like the rose is a hrdaya flower, these are hrdaya foods, meaning "heart healing" in Sanskrit.

Along with being the name of the goddess in your fourth chakra, *kushmanda* is also the name for pumpkin in Sanskrit. Pumpkin is a wonderful Ayurvedic food, traditionally recommended for the fall and winter. Its heavy, nourishing qualities help alleviate heat-related imbalances that can arise from anger, frustration, overwork, overexercise, and too many heating spices in your diet. It is great for your heart. Whenever I eat pumpkin, I feel like I'm filling myself with the essence of joy, love, and laughter, which are the hallmarks of Goddess Kushmanda.

Pomegranates are another powerful heart-healing food. This fruit is considered a superfood in the ancient Ayurvedic tradition (modern science is discovering so much of what the ancients have long known). The Ayurvedic benefits of pomegranates include immune support, brain health, anti-aging properties, digestive elixir, beauty enhancement, and female reproductive health support.

**WAYS YOU CAN RECEIVE POMEGRANATE'S HEALING POWERS:**

- Drink its juice–squeeze its seeds to make it.
- Add it to your food–it goes amazingly on many savory foods.
- Make a face scrub–mix pomegranate peel powder with brown sugar and honey.

Before you benefit from pomegranates, say a prayer of thanks to these great beings for their gifts. Gratitude is the mother of virtues and helps us connect with our mother in nature in a profound way.

**PRACTICE:** *Sing devotional songs (or chant uplifting mantras) aloud.*

Singing is a wonderful way to connect with and heal your heart. It really helps to sing devotional songs, as these directly address divinity and tend to be the most calming and soothing, but you can also listen to any song that resonates within your heart. All love songs can be relistened to as odes to God, in whatever form of divinity you most resonate with. And now you can listen to these songs and sing these songs, knowing that this divinity ultimately lives within you, as your true essence.

Goddess Kushmanda, like Goddess Brahmacharini, holds the japa mala in one of her hands. This is because the mantras you chant on the mala to develop self-control over your mind and senses in the second chakra also help open your heart in your fourth chakra. You can chant those mantras loudly, in a singing way, to really open your heart and heal your emotions.

One incredibly powerful mantra is OM. There is a special yogic breathing exercise called *udgeeth*, meaning "the song of the whale." The whale is the longest-living animal, easily living more than a hundred years, and the secret to its longevity is in how slowly it breathes. Yogic breathing exercises like udgeeth are specifically designed to slow down your breathing and to open and nourish your physical and emotional heart, connecting you with the love that lives within you, in your heart chakra.

To practice, simply close your eyes and focus on your heart as you inhale through your nose. Exhale and hold the *O* sound for three times as long as you chant the *M* sound. Go as slowly with the exhale as you can, to slow down your breathing and expand the quality of your life, as well as the health of your beautiful heart.

PRACTICE: *Make time and space for laughter, and find humor in challenging situations.*

Goddess Kushmanda has a quiet laughter. If you carefully listen to your heart, you will hear her and feel her smiling within your being. To evoke the power of this goddess, it helps to start to see the humor in even challenging situations. When you can find something to laugh about, you start to take situations less seriously and not feel as heavy or depressed about things as they are.

This does not mean faking a smile, laughing when it's inappropriate, or pretending to laugh when you don't actually think something's funny. It simply means being open to humor in your life. You could connect with the power of laughter by reading your favorite comic book or cartoons in the news. You could also watch a funny movie or attend a comedy show.

If you are a naturally humorous person, you can tell jokes. I remember being in the emergency room with my family once when we had to take my father in for a serious health issue. It was the second time he had gone to the hospital in one year. I remember one of my parents' dear friends visiting us late at night and joking that he knew my dad liked the hospital, but he had to stop being such a frequent visitor. The way he said what he did really helped us laugh about the situation and went a long way toward lightening the mood.

### PRACTICE: *Soothe feelings of grief and honor departed loved ones with marigold flowers.*

Marigold is a sacred flower that represents the power and illumination of the golden rays of the sun. Goddess Kushmanda is said to live in the Kingdom of the Sun, and the sun, in the Vedic spiritual tradition, is a symbol of your soul, power, creativity, transformation, courage, and all forms of abundance.

Marigold flowers directly affect your heart chakra. They help clear away the clouds of grief and fatigue we experience in our lives. This flower, used for Día de los Muertos celebrations in Latin American cultures, and for sacred occasions like weddings and funerals, has special antidepressant qualities.

Marigolds are also used to honor the soul dimension of someone you love. In Nepal, there is even an annual festival that honors the undying spiritual love between humans and dogs, where people honor their canine companions with marigold garlands. At times of death, people in India honor the body of those they lose with these garlands. I remember one of my teachers sharing how her grandfather (who was also her spiritual guru) gifted her a marigold flower garland as a way to help her cope with the intense grief she experienced upon losing her mother at an early age. I have personally found a lot of comfort in smelling marigolds during times of immense grief and loss.

You can make a garland of marigolds by sewing them together with a needle and thread. Simply make a tight knot at the end of the thread so the flowers don't fall off, and then push the needle through the thickest part of each marigold stem. You can offer one garland to the image of a deceased loved one whose soul you wish to honor in a sacred place in your home. You can also wear one garland yourself. Inhale its aroma and connect with the light of the radiant sun as you gaze at it while going through times of intense sorrow. It will help you grieve while remembering that Goddess Kushmanda, the bestower of joy within you, is awaiting you, no matter how far away you may feel from her in moments of intense pain.

**Chapter 5**

# Expressing Yourself with Sound and Silence

*The speech without excitement, which is truthful,*
*pleasant and beneficial, and also the practice of sacred study*
*are the practices for conscious speech.*

—BHAGAVAD GITA, chapter 17, verse 15

## Cultivating Expression

There is a curious tension that arises on day 5 of the Navratri practice. On day 4, we practice knowing ourselves, loving ourselves, and developing the personal sovereignty that allows for a healthy relationship with ourselves and others. Those practices then flow into day 5, when we have an opportunity to be with ourselves in silence and to express ourselves to the world through speech.

We best take advantage of that opportunity by embracing and nurturing the child inside us, symbolized by Skanda, the baby who the goddess Skandmata carries. Skanda represents empowerment, and day 5 is about becoming the hero of your own story. Day 5 is an opportunity to combine the fierceness of day 3 and the love of day 4 into a new, more emboldened version of ourselves. On day 5, we feel nurtured, as if we ourselves were the warrior baby. By taking care of ourselves this way, we become more vulnerable, a quality that ultimately allows us to live with greater conviction.

The question becomes how to combine speech and silence into the strongest, most truthful version of who we are and what we believe. In my own case, after nine years of spiritual study in California, I felt more than ready to free the power of my voice when I arrived in New York.

But in order to determine who I was in this liminal space and who I wanted to be in the future, I first needed to immerse myself even more deeply in the sacredness of silence, to connect with the place the Sufi poet Rumi says is "where words are born of silence." Silence has the power to take us to the very core of life, to help us find our own answers, and to connect with the eternal presence of our own soul. In my studies, I learned that silence leads to reflection, reflection leads to conviction, conviction leads to courage, and courage leads to expression.

Without silence, there can be no meaningful expression. And it is important to follow this path because our words have tremendous power. So often words fly out of our mouths. Speech creates karma, and so we must be aware of what we say and how we say it as we move toward the new reality we create on day 5.

As I dug more deeply into how I had allowed myself to be silenced and controlled during the previous nine years, I realized that giving away my voice was rooted in childhood survival mechanisms. To reclaim my power, I had to learn to mother my inner child, honor and care for my own needs, and really radically love myself unconditionally. In doing so, I healed my relationship with my mother, which translated, for me, into no longer unconsciously seeking out authority figures to replay the same disempowering dynamic I had with her in childhood.

In this chapter, we will explore the relationship between sound and silence, and we will learn that there is power—and truth—to be found in both.

## Knowing SKANDMATA

After Durga gives birth to the entire cosmos and grants the power of reproduction to goddesses and then gods, she then takes on the form of a biological mother as Goddess Skandmata. Skanda is the name of this goddess's son, and *mata* means "mother," so *Skandmata* translates as "the mother of Skanda."

Skanda's birth is an interesting story. After Shailputri, the goddess who represents stability, immolates herself in the sacred fire, Shiva, the god who was to become Skandmata's husband, becomes detached from worldly engagements, leading the life of an ascetic and doing intense spiritual practices deep in the Himalayas. At the same time, two demons, Surapadman and Tarakasura, and their minions threaten the gods' existence.

These demons offer a prophecy that only Shiva or a son of his can defeat them. Since Shiva has withdrawn from the world, the demons proceed to wreak havoc given that they believe this prophecy is unlikely to ever be fulfilled. In the meantime, the gods run to Lord Vishnu (god of preservation of the universe), begging him to help them, as they too believe that Shiva won't have a child. But Lord Vishnu tells the gods that they are responsible for the situation, and that Brahmacharini, an incarnation of Shailputri, is destined to be Shiva's wife.

Once Shiva and Brahmacharini are married, their energy combines and produces a seed so fiery that the god of fire must carry it to Saravana Lake. But the heat is so strong that even the god of fire cannot hold it any longer and passes it to the Ganges River, which transports it to Saravana Lake.

Goddess Skandmata then transforms into water itself, as only she could carry Lord Shiva's seed. Skanda is born a handsome, strong, and

powerful youth. He becomes the commander in chief of the army of the gods. He is blessed by all the gods and given special weapons, with which he defeats the demons in a fierce war. Goddess Skandmata is worshipped as the mother of the divinely gifted Skanda.

The story of Goddess Skandmata giving birth to the extremely powerful warrior Skanda is symbolic of the incredible empowerment we all receive when we take time to nurture our inner child. When we do what it takes to heal our negative emotions and speak in a more empowered way, we can give birth to a new version of ourselves and be the heroes of our own lives, like Skanda.

I love connecting with Durga as Skandmata when I feel overwhelmed by emotions and how to best express myself. As someone who found refuge in silence for many years while learning the teachings I share in this book, I struggled initially to release the power of my voice when I became a teacher myself. Remembering that a nurturing and loving mother lives in my throat chakra supported me tremendously in purifying and releasing the shame that held me back from expressing myself completely as I am.

Whether you feel like you need refuge and healing in the sacred space of silence, or that it's time to give voice to something important to you, you can call upon Goddess Skandmata to support you in this process.

## Taking Inventory

Silence is critical to spiritual growth, yet we often perceive silence as something to be avoided. Many people are in the habit of arriving home to an empty room, apartment, or house and immediately putting on podcasts, Netflix, or music. When there is a pause in conversation, our first instinct may be to say the next thing as quickly as possible without allowing time for reflection and discernment. Our world is so filled with noise that we use to distract ourselves from ourselves.

# YOUR VOICE & THE FIFTH CHAKRA

The power of your voice is connected with the fifth chakra (also called the throat chakra). It is located in your throat area. The Sanskrit name for this chakra means pure. This is where your energy, after having been purified through the first three chakras, and then connected with the power of love in the fourth chakra, can express itself. This throat chakra is associated with space and the sense of hearing. Cultivating the power of expression is the gift that this chakra offers you, to speak what is true for you, through sound as well as silence.

Skandmata is depicted as the biological mother of the powerful warrior god Skanda. She rides a lion, yet she is seen breastfeeding her child. Her care for her son represents the possibility that when we care for our inner child, we can become brave and powerful like the spiritual warrior Skanda. It takes bravery, after all, to really speak your truth from a space of knowing what is true for you.

That's why dwelling in silence as you take inventory on day 5 is so important. Our emotions are all there waiting for us, as is the truth about ourselves—what makes us great but also the things about ourselves we might not like or want to change. In silence, we have no choice but to look at ourselves, hopefully with compassion and detachment, and to tend to our emotions as they arise.

I try each week to keep one day to be in complete silence, but even if you don't have the luxury of an entire day, any amount of time can be beneficial and can allow you to connect with your true Self. In silence, the ego subsides, and we remind ourselves not to speak just for the sake of speaking, but to use the interplay between sound and silence to cultivate the power of expression.

In doing so, we can ask ourselves some key questions:

- What emotions does silence bring to the surface for me?

- Have I said anything impulsively that I wish I could take back? What feelings within drove me to do so?

- What negative thoughts repeat themselves on autopilot in my mind?

- Does my speech unite souls or tend to stir up arguments?

- Am I happy with the sound of my voice?

- Do I spend time reading or listening to the sacred words of ancient spiritual texts? How may I incorporate this into my day or week?

There are so many unconscious reasons for why we speak and especially for why we say things we later regret. Before purifying your speech and emotions through silence, it helps to also courageously check in to see if your current communication stems from any of the below:

| | ALWAYS | FREQUENTLY | SOMETIMES | INFREQUENTLY | NEVER |
|---|---|---|---|---|---|
| I lash out at others without thinking. | 1 | 2 | 3 | 4 | 5 |
| I make others feel they are responsible for my feelings. | 1 | 2 | 3 | 4 | 5 |

| | ALWAYS | FREQUENTLY | SOMETIMES | INFREQUENTLY | NEVER |
|---|---|---|---|---|---|
| I spill my unprocessed emotions over others. | 1 | 2 | 3 | 4 | 5 |
| I compare, judge, and put others down to feel better about myself. | 1 | 2 | 3 | 4 | 5 |
| I speak in order to win approval, get attention, or be recognized. | 1 | 2 | 3 | 4 | 5 |
| I gossip to connect with others and fill in awkward silent pauses. | 1 | 2 | 3 | 4 | 5 |
| I speak to manipulate or control someone else's behavior or way of thinking to suit my own agenda. | 1 | 2 | 3 | 4 | 5 |
| I say things to soothe and care for others to secure my relationship with them, instead of speaking what is truthful. | 1 | 2 | 3 | 4 | 5 |

If you scored between 8 and 15 points, purifying your speech is a priority as you move through the Navratri cycle. Doing so will liberate you so much that your new, carefully chosen words will empower you to give birth to a new reality in your daily life.

If you scored between 16 and 30 points, you have good moments and bad moments with your speech and will benefit from constantly asking yourself what is motivating your words and feeding yourself the silence from which conviction of expression emerges.

If you scored between 31 and 40 points, you are embodying conscious speech. Be confident in how you serve as a role model for others in the way you communicate.

# Expressing Yourself with Sound and Silence

Like all of these practices, finding the balance of sound and silence that works best for you is not quick or easy. It may take a week, month, year, or even several years to combine these elements in a way that allows you to know your own truth and express it. Nevertheless, day 5 is a regular opportunity to practice these skills and give yourself the grace and space to combine these elements in your own way.

### Stay quiet.

In the previous section, we used the practice of silence to take inventory. Whatever amount of time you allot for this practice, know that when it is up, there is no need to immediately speak. That certainly does not mean that you should stay silent forever, but also that the spectrum between silence and sound means that you need not choose one or the other.

At the start of my spiritual journey, I found it difficult to practice silence. But over time, I found refuge in it and was able to conserve a great deal of energy, in particular when I began to discern more clearly who was or was not ready to hear what I had to say. Training myself out of an unconscious habit of speaking just for the sake of speaking eventually empowered me to speak the truth that sets us all free. It cut down on confusion and brought me deeper conviction in what I did say when I measured my words and evaluated them in terms of the Bhagavad Gita's conscious speech guidance that I shared at the very beginning of this chapter.

### Listen deeply.

The practice of silence is an opportunity to examine the emotions behind people's words. Words are important, but we can often learn just as much by tuning in to the emotional undercurrent beneath the surface of someone's speech. This is especially important because we tend to re-create relational dynamics in our lives and our speech if we are unwilling to observe and then change them.

As I began to gain insight into my own feelings of shame and fear, I connected them to how my mother had related to me in childhood. When I was sixteen, she told me she saw a lion in my eyes. "I am scared of you," she said. And later, when I started studying Ayurveda, my mother strongly rejected what I was doing. "Why do you have to do all this weird stuff?" she used to ask me, rolling her eyes to express her judgment and disapproval. Although I hadn't realized it at the time, her negativity was far more about her than about anything I was doing.

## Observe your own emotions.

In the silent void of deep listening, I shifted the lens inward. Looking back at my life, I connected patterns of behavior in ways I never had before. At various times, I felt rejected for the strength I had and had unconsciously started to speak in a way that would win the approval of female authority figures. I said things I didn't mean and tried my best to go along with others, making my speech as soft and pleasant as possible. It did not benefit me to communicate this way. Even as it happened, I felt like there was a lump in my throat, or like someone was choking or strangling me, but I continued anyway, hoping the feeling would pass. I also felt ashamed of my body for attracting attention from the opposite sex.

My repressed emotions created a barrier in my relationship with my mother. Throughout my spiritual studies, my mother frequently made it clear that she disapproved of my choices. When I visited home, she cooked my food separately from everyone else's, and she was particularly angry about the way I confronted my father early on in my studies. The way she acted triggered the sense of abandonment I had always felt because she had not protected me from my father or from the sexual abuse of neighbors when I was growing up.

In silence, I observed all the deep emotions that arose within me. Instead of reacting to them, I began to try to understand them. I researched and learned that I had what's known in modern psychology as "the mother wound." It occurs when a mother takes care of a child's physical needs but doesn't give empathy or emotional security. My mother wanted to love me unconditionally, but her conditioning resulted in her only being able to nurture my physical needs. She had always punished me for disagreeing with her, standing up for myself, or expressing pain, sadness, or anger. She used to tell me to stuff my emotions inside, just look pretty and speak pleasantly, no matter what, because that was what she had learned from her own mother. She also blamed the sexual abuse I experienced from neighbors on me.

In silence, I finally understood why I had developed a habit of taking care of others at the expense of my own well-being, as that is what I had learned to do to keep my mother happy when I was a child. Circumstances required me to assume the role of caretaker during my mother's pregnancy with my sister, and beyond that, I did whatever I could to please and care for her. In silence, I understood how getting rejected, shamed for sexual abuse, and having my mother vehemently deny that my father did anything wrong had hurt me so much that I blocked her out of my life for many years and re-created my dynamic with her with others in my early adulthood.

### Beware of projection in your own, as well as others', praise and judgments.

The emotional world of our own self-created projections is called *samsara* in Sanskrit. It is compared to an ocean, because it goes so deep and is so pervasive. When you listen deeply to yourself and others, you will often find that the qualities and actions you admire in others are those you also possess. What we criticize or judge in others is what we often see in ourselves. This is why Edward Wallis Hoch once revealed:

> There is so much good in the worst of us,
>
> And so much bad in the best of us,
>
> That it hardly behooves any of us
>
> To talk about the rest of us.

This goes for others as well. What made my mother's rejection of my "weird ancient ways" more painful was that my Ayurveda family lineage is a maternal one. My mother's father was a renowned Ayurveda healer in India, as were her grandfather, great-grandfather, and so on, tracing back many generations. When I applied the lens of projection to the situation, I was able to not take my mother's rejection so personally. I understood that it was the result of judgments she must have received from her own mother. She didn't have the opportunity to process her emotional trauma and therefore passed it to me. I also understand that a lot of it was her internalized colonial shame, which many native people worldwide carry about our native healing traditions.

I can clearly see now how much my mother abandoned and rejected herself in neglecting to protect me and in initially judging my return to my roots. I reflected parts of my mother that she was not comfortable with in herself.

Furthermore, my mother learned from her mother that female sexuality is shameful and felt that by making me feel shame around my sexuality, she could protect me from getting hurt by men, because I would put up a wall toward them out of shame.

### Choose your words with discernment.

It is essential to consider first if others are ready to hear your message. Will what you have to say have a positive effect on your listener(s) and benefit you as well? In my own case, from the moment I began my spiritual studies, I strongly believed in what I was studying, and I wanted to sing its praises to everyone I met. However, over time, the spiritual practice of silence taught me that people would more likely be drawn to me and to ancient wisdom if I quietly embodied and radiated inner peace.

Consider next if your desires are coloring what you intend to communicate in any way. For example, are you seeking approval for your message? If so, then work to let go of this attachment prior to speaking. This is a lot easier to say than to do, but this way of communicating is empowering and frees you from acquiring additional negative karma through your speech (one of the three seats of incurring karma, along with thoughts and actions).

With every year that passed, I found myself less and less concerned with what my mother thought of my choices. Many times, I thought of trying to heal our relationship, but I still had a wall up between us. Over time, I realized that through my choice to actively care for myself, and stop internalizing shame for sexual abuse I experienced, my mother wound was actually already healed. The way forward wasn't to rehash the past but instead to begin again and to know each other as our authentic selves once and for all. Through a series of conversations, I developed genuine love and compassion for my mother and was also able to give her more time and attention in order to heal the rift between us, without needing to seek her approval.

A few years ago, my mother and I were discussing the concept of spirit animals over text messages. She resonates strongly with peacocks, for their beauty and colors.

"Are you a lion or tiger?" she asked me.

"Lion all the way," I replied. "I am a mountain lion. A mountain lion is like a mother goddess who symbolizes feminine strength, proper use of power, standing behind convictions. Using leadership wisely to bring about truth and goodness. Like Durga's lion. You are always safe with me."

She replied, "You are one in millions to look out for us. Fortunate to have you on board. Jai Mata ji."

*Jai* means "victory." *Mata* means "mother," and *ji* means "respected." The expression, taken together, means "victory to the divine mother."

I was finally able to express my power and advocate for my autonomy by being my own loving mother and extending that love and empowerment to my mother as well. This resolution liberated me to finally advocate for my own needs and feelings, which marked a brave beginning of the next phase of my life during which truly mothering myself is second nature.

The more I found the power and maternal love of Goddess Skandmata within my being, the more I released shame, accepted myself, and started expressing myself authentically, the closer I have grown to my biological mother, and the less abandoned I feel. It meant a lot to me when, during Thanksgiving of the COVID-19 pandemic, my mother even expressed how she wanted to leave my father and come to be with me. At our virtual Thanksgiving dinner, she acknowledged how I am her mother more than she is mine.

I am in awe of the fact that my mother chose to become my student in a one-year Ayurveda Wellness Ambassador Program, never missing a class with me. Her willingness to learn from me reflects her humility. I hope I will be as open to learning from my own children one day as she is now open to learning from me. Today, I find great joy in finding ways to empower my mother's beautiful voice as a singer and by inviting her to teach how to make Ayurvedic recipes on video in my organization's on-line community program. And even though she went through a period of rejecting all that I did to reconnect with my Indian roots through studying Ayurveda, I also feel grateful to her for how she planted seeds in my childhood for me to be proud of the Indian culture I come from (despite my dad wanting us to only speak English and be Westernized).

As long as I remember that I have a goddess within my throat as my mother, who is always there for me and ready to care for me, I feel loved and empowered to continue to give birth to new life that emerges from our speech, emanating from the sacredness of silence.

## The Path Forward: Practices for Expression

PRACTICE: *Tap into sacred silence to reflect on what's most important to you.*

Silence is like Goddess Skandmata, providing the opportunity to give birth to a brand-new reality that can only reveal itself in the void of silence. It is said that silence gives birth to wisdom.

 Silence gives birth to wisdom.

I personally love giving myself at least one full day (usually a weekend day) to be completely silent. I find that I'm able to get totally focused on whatever I need to do and strategize my time in that space of silence. I also love staying quiet in the mornings, and not scheduling phone calls until later in the morning, to reserve a pocket of time each day to be quiet and receptive to whatever insights and emotions arise to the surface. Sitting with a pen and paper in silence helps to capture inspiration and insight that comes up in such a space. I always feel that my inner being gets nurtured by sitting in the womb of silence, which helps me give birth to a new version of reality, informed by the depths of my being.

You can start your practice of silence by carving out a few minutes each day to sit in silence, or perhaps a whole hour or more, working your way up to a full-day personal silent retreat, if you wish, to gain clarity into your innermost being. A prompt for this practice is to ask yourself,

"What do I most value?" It could be wisdom, abundance, beauty, creativity, responsibility, love. For me, the top values on my list are freedom and integrity between thoughts, speech, and actions.

It helps to remember Goddess Skandmata and to ask for her support to care for you in defeating any inner demons that her silence may bring to the surface for you in the process of gaining deep clarity into your true Self.

PRACTICE: *Speak only the truth (abstain from white lies).*

We typically speak lies of all kinds, including white lies, to protect ourselves from the exposure we feel telling the truth would necessitate. But in the ancient Vedic spiritual tradition, there is an expression that means "Truth alone is beautiful." We receive the divine protection of Goddess Skandmata when we surrender to the Truth: discerning the truth behind people and situations and committing to speak only the truth. In the Bible, it is said that "the Truth shall set you free." That's because the voice of your inner conscience always knows when it is violating dharma by speaking lies, no matter how small they may be. We feel empowered by truth, even if it is hard to swallow initially. Lies create suffering, whether we are the ones who speak them or are on the receiving end of someone else's lies.

The barometer for truth that ancient wisdom gives us is that something should withstand the test of time and be true at *all* times: past, present, and future.

So even though you feel angry right now, for example, or have even perhaps struggled with anger your whole life, saying things like "well, I'm just an angry person" may not be true for you or for someone else who struggles with this or another emotion. Our emotions come and go; they do not last. Comments pertaining to your or another person's physical body (like "I'm so fat") are also not true as your body size can change over the course of your lifetime. Even intellectual observations, about how logical a person is, for example, may not hold in all periods of time.

This makes it clear that only the soul and all eternal truths related to the nature of your undying soul are true. The more you speak the truth, the closer you will come to your true Self.

### PRACTICE: *Reflect how what you express benefits you and those you communicate with.*

The Bhagavad Gita, one of the greatest yogic texts, contains advice that ranges from practical to sublime, all geared toward helping us reduce the quantity and increase the quality of our desires. One of the very practical things it advises is how to talk to people in your day-to-day interactions, both personal and professional.

In chapter 17 of the Gita, we learn that one of the best barometers for assessing the effectiveness of what you want to say is whether it is beneficial to both you and to the person(s) to whom you wish to express yourself. For example, you may want to vent your frustration with a friend's lack of responsiveness to your text messages. Normally, this kind of communication is not very beneficial to the other person, though it may feel (temporarily) like a relief to you. But if you apply the Gita's framework to making your speech beneficial, you could reframe your raw complaints into a conversation about how solid friendships can only thrive with good communication on both sides. In that way, you transform a personal attack into a constructive reflection on what the friendship (which both people value) needs to stay strong.

In another instance, you may only consider how you are benefiting the other person by saying what they want to hear, even though doing so does not take into consideration your own feelings.

It takes a lot of courage and effort to examine our communication in the light of how beneficial it is to both ourselves and others. It really helps, therefore, to remember Skandmata in our throats as a nurturing, loving mother who is always there for us, helping us find our bravery to do this inner work.

## PRACTICE: *Speak in a pleasant tone.*

Paying closer attention to the tone of your voice when you speak is a great practice that will help you tune in to your communication in a deeper way and to start aligning your speech with the power of Goddess Skandmata within you. You can say the exact same sentence and have multiple meanings behind your words, depending on the tone of your voice. For example, you can say "thanks a lot" with appreciation, to convey heartfelt gratitude. You could also say "thanks a lot" in a sarcastic, biting tone of voice, which conveys the opposite sentiment.

## PRACTICE: *Pay attention to the emotions behind what you express.*

There is a lot we can learn about ourselves, what we are going through, and what we need to work to let go of simply by observing ourselves and what is going on with us emotionally, underneath the surface of our speech. This is a necessary exercise to first become aware of our emotions and then to let go of negative emotions that do not serve us or the one(s) we are communicating with.

As you speak, pay close attention to what you are actually feeling when you say something to express yourself. For example, we might come across as angry when we're actually trying to cover up our feelings of vulnerability toward someone we really care about. Or we can say something that is "nice" on the surface but inside feel tremendous anger or jealousy. At other times, we may put on an overly confident air through our tone of voice or what we say when we are really feeling quite insecure and unsure of ourselves inside.

The Sanskrit word for the fifth chakra means "pure." Our words create our reality. The more you can identify and let go of negative emotions, the more Goddess Skandmata can come into your speech and help you create a brand-new, more loving reality for yourself and others through the power of your words.

**PRACTICE: *Write a letter honoring any negative emotion or way of speaking that recognizes how it helped you survive and what it prevents you from now.***

Once you have identified which negative emotions you'd like to let go of, it is extremely helpful to write a letter to these feelings. In this way, you acknowledge your emotions and how they impact your speech (and your actions and inactions in life) rather than pretending they don't exist. It is not necessary to beat yourself up about emotions you want to release; instead, you can honor their existence and what felt good about them.

For example, I struggled for a long time with shame. I tried to hide because of it. I would not let anyone see my true Self and tried keeping as quiet as possible. When I look back at this emotion and how it manifested, I recognize the positive aspects of it, in that refusing to be seen or known by others gave me the opportunity to find my true Self without the distractions of other people's attention or talking much with others.

But I also recognized that shame was holding me back. After you have acknowledged your emotions and speech, recognize the ways they have hindered you in your life. In my case, shame kept me from realizing my purpose and sharing the ancient spiritual teachings I was blessed to learn and apply to my own life. In order to be of service, I needed to be visible.

To do this, I closed my eyes and remembered Goddess Skandmata in my heart. One of the beautiful aspects of this maternal goddess is how she can relieve you of all angst, grief, anger, and feelings of victimization for past occurrences in your life. You can actually tell her to release you from these and other negative emotions and patterns of speech. Experience her kindness and compassion as the kindness and compassion you can gift yourself, to heal and purify your emotions.

**PRACTICE:** *Before speaking, consider whether your speech aligns with your core values.*

Defining your core values is an incredibly important exercise. When the journey forward is not clear, values give you a way to carve out your own unique path. Core values are fundamental beliefs that can guide your speech, decisions, and behaviors. Some common examples of core values include honesty, respect, responsibility, service, dependability, commitment, creativity, empowerment, and optimism.

Integrity and freedom are two of my core values; therefore, I constantly assess whether what I do in my own life aligns with what I teach and share with others. This means listening to myself and then making a lot of course corrections. For example, I frequently speak about the importance of digesting not only your food and information but also your emotions and life experiences. This is a process I have worked on in my own life, over time.

Because I value freedom, I am careful to not control others. This can sometimes be very difficult when I wish the best for someone else. For example, I wish my father would take better care of his health, but because I value freedom, I don't tell him what to do. Knowledge is never given; it can only be received when someone is ready to take it. We cannot force anyone to do anything, nor would I wish to do so. I allow my joy to speak for me, whether in words or actions, about how much I benefit from my practices.

**PRACTICE:** *Speak in a way that if your message were to be recorded and echo on for lifetimes, you would be happy with your recording.*

Once you say something, it is nearly impossible to take your words back. You can apologize, yes, but there is no way to undo what you said. Hence, it is essential to consider the consequences of what we say.

The concepts of karma and reincarnation are integral to ancient spiritual traditions. Speech is one of the three ways we create karma (the other two are our thoughts and actions) per the ancient Vedic spiritual tradition. Whatever we speak, somehow, in some way, returns to us, so it helps to consider the impact of our words and how we would feel if we were to hear these words ourselves.

When we engage in our spiritual journey, we have the opportunity to become the best versions of ourselves. This helps ensure that we no longer have to regret things we have said to others. When you contemplate and decide on your words *ahead of time*, you can be happy with not only what you said but also the karmic consequences of your words in times to come. This is what it means to bring purity into your throat chakra.

**PRACTICE:** *Create a personal statement envisioning yourself embodying a more empowered way of expressing yourself.*

First, envision yourself free from negative patterns of speaking and negative emotions. Then, consider and write down what life would be like for you if you were free of what you wish to let go of. What might your face and body look like? What would you do if you were no longer afraid? What new possibilities might exist for you?

Once you have recorded a beautiful new vision for yourself, contemplate what you will need to shift to realize it. What do you need to say yes or no to in order to create more opportunities for feeling at peace with yourself and the way you communicate and express yourself? Do you need to be more silent and to think before you speak? Should you start voicing what comes so clearly through to you?

These questions will lead you to give birth to a more empowered version of yourself. When I answered these questions on my journey, I gave myself several days to do the exercise, to ensure they came from a space deep within me and that I could commit wholeheartedly. I also asked Goddess Skandmata for support in the process, as it takes a lot of courage to commit to changing any part of yourself. It truly is like having a new birth, which is something we want to prepare for by asking for help and guidance from within.

**Chapter 6**

# Defining and Maintaining Healthy Boundaries

*The infinite joy of touching Brahman [supreme consciousness]*
*is easily attained by those who are free of the burden of evil and*
*established within themselves. They see the Self in every creature,*
*and all creation in the Self. With consciousness unified through*
*meditation, they see everything with an equal eye.*

—BHAGAVAD GITA, chapter 6, verses 28–29

## Cultivating Intuition

In the previous chapter, we talked about creating space in your life for sound and silence. In this one, we learn more about how to follow the quiet voice within now that you can hear it.

Each day of the nine-day cycle has a feeling and rhythm, and day 6 is no different. I find this to be a meditative, contemplative day during which my focus on developing and listening to that quiet voice, otherwise known as intuition, leads me deeper into myself and my own experience. It is an opportunity to learn more about who I am but also a chance to understand myself as part of a tapestry of every soul, past, present, and future, that has existed. In this way, I uncover my own divinity as part of the divinity that exists in all of us.

Though each day is distinct, the intuition we cultivate on day 6 is intimately connected with the self-control from day 2 and the love from day 4. These three powers determine the kinds of relationships we have in our lives and govern how we interact with others and with the world. As before, when I speak of relationships, I'm not only referring to romantic relationships or even friendships. I mean our relationship to all beings and to the world itself. The Vedic spiritual tradition teaches that there is just one soul. This means that the true Self in me is the same as that in you, and in every human being, animal, and plant inhabiting this planet.

Over the years, I have also seen the progression from the silence of day 5 to the intuition of day 6 to the truth we discover on day 7. The discernment that occurs on day 6 is critical to the transcendence we uncover on day 7. Day 6 is an opportunity to examine the opposing ideas and viewpoints that exist in our lives and to find a way to reconcile them with what we learn about ourselves when we begin to trust our own intuition.

This is particularly important in a world full of stories and ideas we may have about ourselves, many of which are simply not true. So often, we can be on the receiving end of gaslighting, in which someone tries to deny our reality and our experience of the world even when our intuition says the opposite. But our truth is an intuitive realization that comes about through the work we do, so it is essential to listen to our inner voice and follow where it leads. As I've said before, this process is not instantaneous but will become more natural each time you arrive at this important part of the Navratri cycle.

# AWAKENING YOUR INNER GURU

The word *guru* means "the remover (*gu*) of darkness (*ru*)." This darkness is not literal, but rather it is a metaphor for the suffering we experience due to dark emotions like fear, anger, and jealousy. In the Vedic spiritual tradition, it is believed that all the suffering we experience in life is due to lack of spiritual knowledge of who we really are as eternal, all-powerful souls. Though the word *guru* is now commonplace as a label for any expert, in the spiritual field, a guru is someone who removes the darkness of ignorance by teaching you through an example of awakened spiritual consciousness. In the ancient Vedic spiritual tradition, the goal of education is for a student to become a guru. When this happens, the guru typically blesses and bids the student farewell. The student gratefully moves on to continue living according to the guru's teachings and to share the guru's wisdom in the world as a guru themselves. This is how the unbroken chain of spiritual lineages has carried on from the beginning of time until today.

In this chapter, we will come to know the brave Goddess Katyayani, who cuts away the parts of our lives that separate us from ourselves. We'll also learn about ancient conflict resolution strategies that still work today and allow us to define boundaries so that our intuition is available to us not just when we create the silence that allows us to hear it but also on every day, and in every moment, of our lives.

# Knowing KATYAYANI

On the sixth day of Navratri, Durga emerges as the descendant of Sage Katyayan, who had no children but who observed spiritual disciplines for many years, which brought him a daughter, known as Katyayani. She was created as a fighter to put a stop to the damage being done by a great demon who caused trouble for the gods.

Katyayani is known as the wish-fulfilling aspect of the mother goddess Durga. She holds one of her hands out in a gesture of fearlessness and another in a gesture of blessing. Her sword cuts away the great demon of fear that keeps us separate from our divinity. She supports you to exercise discernment in terms of the right desires to set in your heart—ones of the highest quality.

Whereas Goddess Brahmacharini deals with the physical aspect of relationships, Goddess Katyayani deals more with the emotional and intellectual side. This includes all relationships, not just romantic ones. She is, however, worshipped by young girls in India for her boon-fulfilling aspect of granting good husbands. What's important to note here is that you should not evoke the power of Goddess Katyayani simply to find a partner from a place of desperation, but rather so that the divine will come to you as your partner. Her lesson for all of us is that we should have very high standards for the type of partner we want to have, and what kinds of relationships we, more generally, want to welcome into our lives.

As someone who was pressured from an early age to marry the kind of person my parents would approve of, I loved learning about Goddess Katyayani and made her my role model for keeping my standards high. I also feel it is very important for those on a spiritual journey to connect with the divinity in their partners, as well as all others in your life. The key to connecting with the divinity within you in your third eye (where

Goddess Katyayani lives within you) is knowing how to create clear boundaries with others that will allow you to ultimately honor your own intuition, first and foremost. Having high standards may also mean embracing being alone. Being alone and being lonely are two very different things. You can feel lonely in relationships and feel very happy alone. After all, it is when you get to a place of feeling genuinely very happy alone that you can attract a higher vibration partner, which Goddess Katyayani is believed to bless us with.

## YOUR INTUITION & THE SIXTH CHAKRA

The power of intuition is connected with your sixth chakra (called the "third eye"). Its location is said to be in between your eyebrows. This is where you access your inner wisdom and deeper knowing about who you are as an eternal, spiritual being. This sixth chakra is associated with light. Cultivating the power of intuition by opening your third eye brings you the gift of insight and clarity so that you may navigate darkness in your life.

Katyayani is depicted as holding a lotus in one hand and a sword in another, with one of her hands in the gesture of fearlessness and the other in the gesture of granting blessings. She is said in ancient Vedic spiritual mythology to be the goddess who grants our high-quality, well-contemplated desires, provided we clear our hearts of fear (which blocks blessings from reaching us). She helps us specifically in our many relationships in life and helps to experience divine unity with others.

# Taking Inventory

Defining and maintaining boundaries is a critical skill for building and nurturing healthy relationships, but it's particularly important to set boundaries when dealing with narcissists in your life. Narcissists tune in to naturally empathetic people and their vulnerabilities. They may purposely cause you to question your intuition and, hence, your reality. It is, therefore, essential to know how to spot them.

Western psychologists reveal how there are typically "three E's" involved with narcissism: exploitation, entitlement, and empathy impairment. Here is a list of telltale signs to look for when someone makes you doubt your intuition and violates your boundaries.

**Does this person habitually:**

1.  Dominate your conversations, which are always centered around themselves?

2.  Break rules and social norms (e.g., transgressing physical boundaries, cutting in lines, stealing groceries, disobeying traffic laws)?

3.  Disrespect other people's physical space, thoughts, feelings, and possessions?

4.  Project a false image of themselves with objects, status, people, and achievements to make you believe they are worthy of admiration (which they seem to never get enough of)?

5.  Blame you for their own mistakes?

6.  Make you believe you cannot live without them because of how special they are?

7. Twist information in a way that harms you and protects them, while making you question your reality and feel that you must be crazy?

8. Expect you to drop everything you are doing and your needs to serve them at their every beck and call?

9. Make you feel inferior to them or throw tantrums when you dare to disagree with them?

10. Manipulate you into serving their needs by guilting you about how much they've given you in the past or by presenting themselves as a victim you should feel compelled to make unreasonable sacrifices for?

## Defining and Maintaining Healthy Boundaries

Vedic spiritual tradition offers us an ancient four-part conflict resolution strategy intended to help us trust our intuition and protect our reality. In this section, I will teach you this practice so that you may use it in your own life when conflict arises between the world within you and the world outside you.

### 1. Shama (pacification)

In this first step, ancient Vedic spiritual tradition calls upon us to try to resolve any dispute through amicable means. *Pacification* means calming the other person down and developing a common understanding of the situation that caused the conflict.

### 2. Daana (donation)

If you cannot achieve reconciliation, the next step is *daana*, meaning "donation." The tradition advises us that during this second step we should give or let go of something, such as a gift, either literal or something figurative, like pride. It also means being willing to accept another's apology.

Above all else, we understand daana as a peace offering or a conciliatory gesture that will allow for the cessation of conflict (not necessarily the continuation of the relationship if we discern that it is not good for us).

### 3. Bheda (separation)

If neither an attempt at reconciliation nor a peace offering succeeds at mending the conflict, then the next step is to ask for separation that allows everyone time away from the heat of the situation to reflect on the way forward. It is interesting to consider that even in ancient times, people used the same kinds of strategies that we do today to resolve disputes and that they understood the need for distance to discern the best course of action. I think of *bheda* as pressing the pause button on a relationship in the hope that clarity will emerge from a deeper intuitive understanding of the situation.

One interesting aspect of this conflict resolution strategy is how separation is the third, not the first, step. I have met many people who see separation as the way to resolve conflict. While I understand that feeling, I do believe there is wisdom in trying first to achieve a peaceful resolution even as I recognize now that one cannot try to reconcile *indefinitely* at the cost of one's own inner peace.

### 4. Danda (punishment)

When none of the previous steps work, the ancients advise us to proceed to *danda*, or "punishment." Then and now, there were situations that individuals could not resolve or handle on their own, situations that, despite our best efforts, escalate into physical or psychological danger even after a period of separation designed to cool hot tempers and settle hurt feelings. In the case of danda, we are advised to ask for help from an impartial party or intervention from a higher authority. Imagine something like calling the police or getting a restraining order, and you can understand the intensity and urgency of danda.

Though our first impulse might be that "conflict resolution" always means repairing a relationship, it might also mean ending the relationship in a way that honors both parties but also acknowledges the truth of the situation, which is that a reconciliation is not desirable, healthy, or possible.

In practicing these principles in my own life, I have found them to be a useful guide so that I am able to embody courage in the face of fear and find my inner light in the face of dark outer situations. I don't believe that boundaries need to be cold, sharp, and prickly like thorns. Rather, I believe in "fragrant boundaries," which are limits through which we can assert ourselves with strong actions that are guided by a pure heart and wishes for the highest and best for others. Though I feel lucky to have had few of these dramatic moments, when they occur, I now feel Goddess Katyayani within me. I also understand her sword in a more nuanced way; not only does it cut away the people in our lives who do not serve or see the vision of our higher selves that we seek to achieve, but it also cuts away fears and fearful attachments, which keep us bound to our small selves.

# The Path Forward: Practices for Intuition

PRACTICE: *Spend less time with people who deplete you energetically.*

It really makes a difference to observe how you feel around different people in your life. Are there some people who energize you while others drain your energy and make you tired and relieved to no longer be in their presence? Be honest with yourself in answering these questions, as doing so will help you discern how much time and energy to offer to different people in your life.

It is not easy to tune in to the inner voice of your intuition when you are surrounded by people who try to dissuade you from believing in what you feel to be true. Often when you try to share spiritual insights with those who are not on a spiritual path, they may tease you about it (at best) or outright invalidate your intuition. To protect your intuition, therefore, you need to use Katyayani's powerful sword to cut away situations that might cause you to lose trust in yourself and your spiritual journey. You must also let go of the need to win the approval of everyone in your life.

Family members can be very challenging to deal with when you're on a spiritual journey. You can effectively set limits with them and others who are important to you but don't understand your spirituality by sharing that you need a certain amount of time to do whatever it is that inspires you spiritually and sharing when you are available outside of that. Doing this is not selfish; it is helping you connect with the best part of you, so that when you return to your relationships, you will feel energized and be the best you can be for others this way too.

Deciding to spend less time with people who take away from you energetically is not something to do out of cruelty or hatred for those in your life. You can be completely kind and loving to such people while simply choosing to make yourself less available to them. Shifting your energy away from people who deplete you gives you more space to nurture yourself with people, projects, and energy that make you feel good about yourself. Feeling good about yourself, in turn, awakens your trust in the inner knowing in your third eye, allowing the light of Goddess Katyayani to shine within your being.

## PRACTICE: *Spend time doing solitary activities.*

Solitude is essential to be able to go inward, and going inward is the key to activating the power of your intuition, which can be accessed only from within you. Even if you can't always be completely alone, it helps to spend time each day doing introverted activities like reading spiritual books, writing in a journal, or going for a solitary walk outdoors.

As you become more introverted, you will find that you have fewer reactions to others, which makes it difficult for others to provoke you. This lessens relationship conflicts that are based in reactive words and behaviors. By engaging in spiritual practices to enhance your intuition and awaken your third eye, you can feel more confident about navigating challenges that arise in your relationships by staying closer to your true Self.

### PRACTICE: *When giving to others, do so in a way that helps them grow.*

Giving is a wonderful activity, but the truest gift comes from understanding that nothing in the world can give you the joy you are looking for, as this can be found only in connecting with your true Self.

Goddess Katyayani inspires us to give in such a way that we do not inspire others to become dependent upon us. This is because independence is the ultimate goal of the spiritual journey. If we give in a way that makes others dependent on us, we take away their sovereignty and ultimately do them a disservice.

Victor Hugo shares a beautiful story in *Les Misérables* about how true giving can benefit the recipient. One night, a convict escapes prison and must find a place to sleep. A priest welcomes him, feeds him, and lets him sleep at his home. The convict accepts the hospitality but steals a couple of silver plates in the middle of the night. When a police officer catches the convict, the priest protests, questioning the officer as to why he is harassing the convict and claiming to have gifted the plates to him. The policeman apologizes for his mistake and goes away. When he is gone, the priest picks up two pure silver candlesticks and gives them to the convict. He tells him: "Remember, life is to give, not to take." The convict leaves a changed man and transforms into a giver from that day forward.

We want our giving to have this kind of impact upon others, wherein we model for them the path to becoming a nobler, more independent person (both emotionally and otherwise) by walking that path ourselves.

**PRACTICE:** *Treat others the way you wish to be treated.*

The ancient Vedic spiritual tradition upholds the law of causation, which has two facets: the law of destiny and the law of karma. Who you are today is a culmination of all the past thoughts, desires, and actions you have had. You reap the seeds you sow according to this law of destiny. Hence, your current destiny is fixed, determined by the actions you have taken in the past. As the Upanishads, an ancient Vedic spiritual text, inform us, destiny works in this manner:

> *Sow a thought, reap an action.*
> *Sow an action, reap a habit.*
> *Sow a habit, reap a character.*
> *Sow a character, reap a destiny.*

> You are the architect
> of your own destiny.

You are the architect of your own destiny, which begins at the level of your thoughts. The law of karma takes the law of destiny forward into the future. It extends further to affirm that you are not only a product of your past, but that you have the power to produce your future. There is nothing you can do about the past, so it's important to let go of worrying about it. But with regard to your future, you are a master. You can create a brighter future for yourself in relationships by treating others the way you would like to be treated.

This practice goes along with the power of leading others by example. The best way to plant seeds for happier relationships is by getting clear on what you would like to see more of (respect, love, appreciation, and so on) in your relationships, and then giving more of that to yourself. We have to give love to receive it. This is Goddess Katyayani's message for us in our third eye of inner wisdom and knowing.

**PRACTICE:** *Look into your own eyes and see the divine in you.*

It is often easier to see divinity in the images of gods and goddesses and in the faces of people we look up to. For those of us actively engaged in serving others, it may be easier to see divinity reflected in the eyes of children, elders, and even animals and plants. For a long time, on my own spiritual journey to know my Self, I put others before myself. I could see the divinity within those I looked up to as teachers because I placed them on a pedestal, while not owning my own self-worth. I only felt good about myself to the extent I gave to others and performed actions that were unselfish, for others' benefit.

But the presence of Goddess Katyayani in my third eye helped wake me up to the fact that if my aim was to see the unity of all beings, then I could not leave myself out of that oneness. In a sense, studying the spiritual Self is really a beautiful invitation to be kinder to yourself en route to learning and embodying the full spiritual power of who you really are. By looking into your own eyes and seeing Goddess Katyayani (or any other form of divinity you most resonate with) reflected in them, you have an opportunity to experience a profound kind of self-love. The eyes, where this goddess lives, are very powerful on the spiritual journey, because they are mirrors of your soul.

When you really look into someone's eyes, even when you are angry with them, you can see yourself reflected, literally and figuratively. Even if you are angry or frustrated with yourself for some reason, or especially if you are feeling unworthy of love, it helps to look into your own eyes and forgive yourself. Love yourself. See the light of the goddess in your own eyes. The aim of the spiritual journey is to see the same Self in all beings. When you can first start seeing the light of the divine in your own eyes, it will deeply change how you see everything—and everyone—in your life for the better.

PRACTICE: *Practice forgiveness with discernment and healthy boundaries.*

Anger is a necessary emotion that informs us when our boundaries have been transgressed, but forgiving others for the ways they hurt us is an important part of the practice of loving others. Most important, doing so is a way to love ourselves by not punishing ourselves with the damaging effects of anger, which ruin our happiness.

There is a wonderful ancient Vedic parable of a serpent and a sage that brings home this message. A serpent lived outside a village, attacking villagers and injecting them with its poisonous venom.

One day a sage passed by the serpent. It came out of its hiding place, about to strike. Unlike most passersby, the sage stood completely still, undisturbed.

The serpent recognized the divinity in the sage and asked for forgiveness. The sage responded by recommending that the serpent not be so full of hatred and cruelty. And that he stop stirring up so much trouble in the village. The serpent agreed to drop its aggression and live peacefully with others.

A few days later, the sage came by again. He found the serpent wounded and defeated. He asked the serpent why it had lost all its power. The serpent responded: "Sir, I just followed your wise guidance. I expressed my love to everyone. The villagers threw stones at me." The sage said, "I'm sorry. I should have clarified. I wanted you to live in harmony with others but not to the point of letting others attack. Without feeling hatred in your heart, you should have hissed and sent people away."

This story has been a huge key to unlocking my own spiritual freedom. My spiritual name is Ananta, which means "king of the Naga serpents." When I first began my spiritual journey, there was such an emphasis on loving others, to my own detriment. As I progressed on my path, I realized how important it was to apply discernment everywhere, with everyone, all the time.

Some of the most powerful moments of personal transformation have been when I had to hiss away manipulative people who were very close to me. I had to first find a pure space within, and then feel my Oneness with and love for these people in my heart while acting for the greater good (dharma). Forgiveness is much more empowering than anger and revenge, which only serve to escalate and prolong the pain of conflict, rather than allowing you to experience the inner peace that Goddess Katyayani reveals in your third eye as your true nature.

## PRACTICE: *Create a sacred sanctuary space where you can access your intuition.*

Your intuition is the voice of Goddess Katyayani speaking directly to you. It really helps to create a special sacred space where you can go to tune in to this inner guidance of the divine within. You can fill your sacred space with different symbols that speak directly to you and remind you of the highest in you. Photographs, statues, letters, crystals, gemstones, spiritual books, drawings, paintings, incense, candles, and all other kinds of sacred artwork are amazing ideas for what you can add to your sanctuary.

I keep statues of Goddess Lakshmi and Goddess Saraswati, along with one of the elephant god Ganesha (who works with Lakshmi), in my sanctuary space, which is presently a bookshelf turned into an altar. I also keep a japa mala (rosary beads); kalash (copper vessel); sacred books; a photo of Mother Mary; a photo of my guru Baba Ayodhya Nath Sinha; his father and teacher, Bade Baba Shanti Prakash; and some plants in my sacred space. All of these particular beings and things remind me to tune in to the power and knowing that live inside me. I personally love to look at them while I work, as they help me align my thoughts, speech, and actions.

When you connect with sacred symbols and beings, you help your inner sanctuary, your inner spiritual home, find a home in the outer world. When I look at Goddess Lakshmi on my altar, for example, I remember the power of love and abundance within me. When I see Goddess Saraswati, I am reminded of my higher knowledge and wisdom. Seeing the kalash reminds me of the ability I have to cleanse myself. And so on. By creating your own sacred sanctuary space, you can connect with symbols that have been imbued with energy and meaning over centuries. You also give yourself an opportunity to tap into ancient wisdom and spiritual grace, the power of Goddess Katyayani in your third eye of intuition.

PRACTICE: *Keep a dream diary to observe repeated signs, symbols, or messages from within.*

Your dreams can be full of inner guidance from deep within your subconscious being. They contain within them different signs and symbols that serve as clues to your next steps and potential destiny. Write down what you see in your dreams each morning when you awaken. Even if you can't quite remember everything, you may recall just enough detail that you can start to observe patterns. As you keep this diary, notice if patterns emerge in terms of recurring people, signs, symbols, or messages that your subconscious may be trying to communicate to you.

PRACTICE: *Notice synchronicities of repeated messages, symbols, numbers, and animals in your waking life and investigate their deeper meanings.*

Staying awake and alert to the presence of different signs, symbols, significant numbers, and animals in your waking life is a profound practice. It helps to also write down what you observe in a journal to start to see if there is repetition. You can then learn more about what you observe, or even a particular symbol or animal you resonate with. This practice is especially beneficial when you are confused about something major in your life (like a relationship, path of study, or your career). It can also be instrumental for making decisions, like whether or not to move, start a new job or business, get married, have children, and so on.

Lions are an animal I deeply resonate with. I have always loved Simba and found his journey in *The Lion King* to reflect my own journey. In investigating lions further, I learned that I resonated specifically with the cougar. In researching them on SpiritAnimal.info, I found: "If cougar has approached you, it is an indication you have come into your own power. Now is the time to take the lead of a situation. Now is the time to be strong."

In addition, I learned on SpiritAnimal.info that "cougar is here to remind us to balance our power. It is important to know when to be gentle and when asserting your energy will be more productive. Perhaps the most important lesson we learn from this power animal is how to use our leadership qualities without the presence of ego. Cougar strengthens your connection with the spirit world and strikes fear in even the bravest of hearts. You can prevail against all odds, and you are the monarch of your domain."

Words connected with cougar: *mother goddess, standing behind convictions, messenger between human and divine beings, sensory evaluation, spiritual warrior, enigma.* I actually began writing this book right when I was observing the cougar's presence in my dreams, to strengthen my own intuitive connection with Goddess Durga in her nine forms during the nine nights of Navratri.

**Chapter 7**

# Transcending Trauma with Wisdom

*The supreme One, who is self-controlled and peaceful, is balanced in cold and heat, in pleasure and pain, as also in honor and dishonor.*

—BHAGAVAD GITA, chapter 6, verse 7

*Happy are the spiritual warriors, who get such a battle that comes unsought, as an open door to heaven.*

—BHAGAVAD GITA, chapter 2, verse 32

## Cultivating Transcendence

After we have defined and protected our reality with our intuition on day 6, it is necessary to ensure it becomes aligned with the Ultimate Reality, the Truth, which withstands the test of time. Aligning our reality with the Ultimate Reality means letting go of any attachments to old stories we have told and experienced so we can simply hold on to only that which is eternal and changeless. On day 7, we start to see everything with the eyes of wisdom, which can cut to the core of every situation.

# WHAT IS THE ULTIMATE REALITY?

Ultimate Reality, or Truth (with a capital *T*), is another term for the one universal consciousness that is believed in the Vedic spiritual tradition to hold all beings and things together. For something to reflect Truth or Ultimate Reality, it must remain the same in all times: the past, present, and future. In that sense, the only thing that stands the test of time and qualifies as Ultimate Reality is the eternal nature of the soul. Only the soul (that is the same in all beings) remains unaffected and unchanged by the passage of time. The more we study spirituality, the more we begin to align our existence with this Ultimate Reality and make decisions that bring us closer to that which is eternal in life.

I find a lot of similarity between Goddess Kalaratri, who symbolizes the spiritual power of transcendence, and Goddess Chandraghanta, who represents the power of transformation (in chapter 3). While transformation happens from taking strong, consistent action to overcome our fears, transcendence results from applying spiritual knowledge to see traumas we have experienced through the eyes of wisdom. This ensures we never see ourselves as helpless victims at the mercy of a cruel world but rather as powerful manifesters of our own destinies.

Goddess Kalaratri is undeniably fierce and ferocious in every possible way. She shows us that we transcend trauma when we are willing to dispel the illusions in which we were previously (unconsciously) invested. This battle is only possible once we have become steady with the previously acquired powers of stability, creativity, transformation, love, voice, and intuition.

Despite Goddess Kalaratri's frightening appearance, I find her to be the most loving form of Goddess Durga because she removes everything that is *not* us: the illusions, lies, and myths we have subscribed to (without even knowing we have done so!). Because only when we are free from illusions are we truly free. This goddess brings the Gospel of John to life: "And you shall know the Truth, and that Truth shall set you free."

Vedanta spiritual philosophy describes how Truth, to be true, must be so at all times: past, present, and future. It also defines the world as *dvandvas*, a Sanskrit word meaning "pairs of opposites." When confronted with pleasure and pain, we humans are conditioned to run toward pleasure and away from pain. True yogis, however, wait for pain and difficulty, because it is only in facing pain, sorrow, and dishonor that we have the opportunity to transcend the duality of pleasure and pain and, hence, transcend the world and the traumas it gives us (based on our past karma). The spiritual practice of transcending the pairs of opposites is called *titiksha* in Sanskrit. It is the key to our spiritual evolution.

Transcending the world does not mean sitting alone in a cave somewhere. It means developing what Lord Krishna describes in chapter 2 of the Bhagavad Gita as *stitha pragya*, meaning "steady wisdom." This comes from transcending desire and its associated fears (of not getting what we want or losing what we have that we wanted so much) and anger (what we experience when our desires are thwarted).

To develop steady wisdom, we must be anchored at all times, as much as possible, in knowledge of what is eternal. With this anchoring, we can practice discernment between the eternal and transient.

Knowledge is power. It arms us with all kinds of weapons we need to become true spiritual warriors, like Goddess Kalaratri. Gaining even more knowledge at the emotional, spiritual, and physical levels was the key to transcending the trauma I endured in the past, on my journey toward becoming a spiritual warrior. The deeper I dug into understanding each trauma I faced, the more I learned from both darkness and light. Why then attach a value judgment to one or the other?

# Knowing KALARATRI

Goddess Kalaratri is, by far, the most terrifying form of Goddess Durga. *Kal* means "time" in Sanskrit. It also means "death." *Ratri* means "night," "darkness" (of the night), and "ignorance" (when you are unable to see the Truth). Goddess Kalaratri is the one who brings about death of the dark night of ignorance of who you are as a spiritual being.

This goddess is depicted as being dark blue, like the night sky, with wild, disheveled hair. She has four hands and carries a scimitar and a thunderbolt, which Lord Indra gifts to her and which bring about goodness. Her other two hands are in gestures of giving (blessings) and protection (from fear). She has three eyes. Fire emerges from her nostrils when she breathes. She wears a mala (collection, typically of beads) of electricity-like energy.

Once upon a time, two demons, Shumbha and Nishumbha (who were responsible for sending the great demon to attempt to seduce Goddess Katyayani), received a prophecy that no male, human or animal, would ever defeat them. They could only be defeated by a woman. They did not know any female powerful enough to kill them, so this prophecy gave them license to do whatever they wanted. They began by torturing saints and insisting the saints worship them instead of divine beings. They also sent two other demons, Chanda and Munda, to fight Chandi, a powerful goddess. In the heat of battle, Chandi created another goddess, Kalaratri, to help her fight them off.

After Kalaratri defeated Chanda and Munda, Shumbha and Nishumbha sent yet another demon, called Raktabeej, to kill Kalaratri. *Rakta* means

"blood" and *beej* means "seed." Raktabeej had the power of cloning so that whenever a single drop of his blood fell to the ground, it served as a seed from which another demon like him would suddenly appear.

When Kalaratri saw she was not going to be able to kill Raktabeej so long as his blood fell to the ground, she started to drink the blood herself to prevent it from becoming another clone, and thereby eventually won the fierce battle.

According to the mythology, Kalaratri destroys all evildoers and thereby has the power to put to rest long-standing issues of cruelty and abuse. She is the ultimate mother goddess, who rewards those who follow her (by following the highest Truth) by removing illusions from her devotees. Initially, she is not easy to look at, just as the Truth is not always easy for us to see. But when we do finally open our eyes, the Truth liberates us from the bondage and suffering we experience by subscribing to illusions.

I personally found Kalaratri very intimidating initially. I didn't really understand her until I started to look deeper at myself and the conditioning I had subscribed to throughout my life, like the idea that the love and approval that others could offer me was greater than my own. She gave me the strength to see what was transient and changing in my life, versus that which is eternal and unchanging (the soul of all beings). Once I could see these illusions, they vanished. And all I was left with was my true Self.

This goddess is the emblem of spiritual enlightenment in many ways. Enlightenment does not come without a fierce battle against the darker forces, thoughts, and emotions within yourself. The spiritual journey is the hardest one you will ever embark upon, but it is also the one that gives you the greatest gifts, which stay with you not only in this lifetime but in lifetimes to come. No progress on the spiritual path ever goes to waste. Goddess Kalaratri is someone we can call upon as we engage in our own deeper battles for the power of true, eternal love (versus transient attachments) to prevail in our lives.

## TRUTH & THE SEVENTH CHAKRA

The power of Truth is connected with the seventh chakra (known as the crown chakra). It is located at the crown of your head. This is where spiritual energy leaves your body at the time of death. This is also where you begin to experience enlightenment. Cultivating the power of Truth in your crown chakra empowers you to move into a more enlightened state of being, wherein you can experience the interconnectedness of your own soul with the universal soul.

Kalaratri is depicted as a terrifying goddess, full of fierceness, with a japa mala (rosary, usually made of prayer beads) made of intense, electricity-like energy. Her hair is disheveled and all over the place. She rides a donkey. She is not that easy to see! This is symbolic of how Truth, while it ultimately sets you free, is not easy to look at initially, when it's not sugarcoated and wrapped in layers of lies and illusions. But when you are finally able to see reality for what it is, you realize it's the greatest gift.

## Taking Inventory

How do you know you are evolving spiritually? There are three main signs you are developing stitha pragya, steady wisdom, in the face of triggering situations that remind you of previous traumas in your life. They center around the mental agitations you experience when you have desire, fear, or anger.

It was extremely helpful to use these signs as a guide for myself when I went through painful experiences along my spiritual journey, especially when the actions of others triggered my childhood pain. I have noticed that each time these situations arise, I am more able to move through my emotional reactions swiftly and with less intensity, rather than remain in a painful and unresolved state as I would have earlier in my life.

Signs your own wisdom is becoming steadier:

1. The frequency of your mental agitation in the face of triggering situations reduces.

2. The intensity of your pain when triggered is less than before.

3. Your recovery time from a triggering situation is faster than before.

## Transcending Trauma with Wisdom

*Determine what underlying emotional desire(s) may have led you to play a role in any trauma you experienced as an adult and see through them by understanding the illusion(s) inherent in them.*

Because we are creatures of patterns, unless we boldly own our part in re-creating familiar patterns, we will keep repeating the same dynamics within different relationships. To create pattern-breaking changes, we must bravely look at the desires that cause us to give away our power.

In my case, I came to recognize two strong desires within myself. One was a deep yearning for unconditional maternal love. The other was to know my true Self.

As I reflected on the ways in which my desire for motherly love was at the root of much of the trauma I experienced, I saw through the illusion that the love of a mother was something I needed to find outside of myself. The spiritual journey of Navratri had brought me to a sublime experience of the divine in the form of not just one but nine different mothers I could find by looking deep within. When I simply remember that a loving mother goddess lives inside me, I remember that I have the power to be my own mother and care for the child within me who wants her mother's love and protection at all times.

### Gain spiritual knowledge in a systematic way to remember and attach to your own eternal soul.

The only thing that can truly fill the emotional void within ourselves is an abiding armor of connection with our true Self. This type of emotional sovereignty is the quest of the spiritual journey and is made possible by knowing who we are as eternal beings. The path of liberation and transcendence is a deeply spiritual one.

While the word *guru* may be triggering to some, due to gurus who have used the power of the title to abuse people, a true guru is one who awakens the guru in others. There is a Sanskrit word, *vishvasi*, that means being willing to put faith in trustworthy sources and not be bitten by cynicism beyond reasonable boundaries. I feel so blessed to have studied (and to continue to study) the Bhagavad Gita and many other Vedanta texts systematically with a true guru in Swami Parthasarathy.

In *Vedanta Treatise*, Swamiji (as he is affectionally called) teaches students to question everything. Doing so develops your subtle intellect, which empowers you to discern what is eternal and true from what is transient and false, an essential practice to propel us forward on the spiritual journey. In this way, we come to realize who we are more and more and to forget who we are less and less often. Systematically learning who we really are, contemplating this knowledge, and then acting in a way that reflects the knowledge of our true Self is, to me, the essence of spiritual awakening. Questioning everything we do also empowers us to approach our actions with greater intentionality and to change our behaviors toward others we are in positions of leadership with (like children, students, employees, etc.), so we do not blindly repeat unconscious behaviors of our parents, teachers, bosses, and others.

In the face of the trauma I experienced when I had years of spiritual study behind me, it was ultimately the knowledge of who I am that empowered me to see through illusions other people presented of themselves and to save myself from danger and distress. This knowledge continues to connect me directly to my power and gives me confidence to transcend my ego's comfort zone in service of Truth and the greatest good of all (dharma).

The more I know and remember who I am as a spiritual being, especially during dark and difficult times, the more empowered I feel, and the less anyone outside me has the power to hurt me. When I view the traumas of my life through the lens of transcendence, I can see how everything I experienced was a portal for my awakening to the unquestionable power of my true Self.

This perspective of trauma ensures that I never see myself as a victim of others' dark behaviors. Instead, I view traumatic events as initiations or rites of passage that I constantly choose to transcend rather than repeat in my mind or life. I do this by deepening my knowledge of who I am as a spiritual being. Today, when I remember all the traumas I experienced, I see them as profound teachers that led me back to knowing and attaching only to my true Self: the sole purpose of a spiritual quest.

### Gain physical strength as a way to embody the power of a warrior.

Once you gain insight into your unconscious emotional desires and use systematic spiritual knowledge to transcend these desires (the essence of the inner warrior path), it is important to then embody this power physically. We store trauma in our bodies; hence, it is important to move the body in order to move the emotions and allow them to flow instead of staying stuck. I personally find martial arts to be a fantastic avenue

for embodying my inner warrior self outwardly. If you're unable to do intense physical strength training, however, even engaging in something like assertiveness training (to fully express yourself) can connect you with the power of transcendence.

I personally learned Kalaripayattu ("Kalari" for short). Kalari is the world's most ancient form of martial arts and one of the greatest forms of *atma rakshana*, or "protection of the eternal soul." Kalari's aim is healing and protection of the self, and even your "enemy," as it is rooted in the belief that there is actually no other. There is only one Self, and hence, the only real enemies we have are the inner demons that hold us separate from our true Self.

It is said that the power of Goddess Durga is equivalent to the power of all the male gods. The male gods give Durga their weapons to destroy the greatest demon, whom they cannot conquer. Learning Kalari was and is a deeply empowering spiritual practice for me to physically embody the power of Goddess Durga. It has given me the strength to be visible and outwardly express myself instead of keeping everything I have and all that I am bottled inside.

The worries of the past and the anxieties we have for the future are what prevent us from living fully in the present moment: an essential spiritual practice of transcendence. I have no control over the sexual abuse I experienced and was blamed for in the past. I accept it all as karma and consciously choose to see it as my invitation to experience my inviolable spiritual power. Embodying the strength of a warrior and continuously engaging in training to quickly strategize blocking and defending my body from various situations I encountered in the past, until it becomes second nature, gives me the courage to transcend the pain of the past and feel fully alive in the now, without getting anxious about future threats.

At every level, emotionally, spiritually, and physically, embodying the power of transcendence gives us the strength to rise above our deepest fears and live free, here and now, eternally.

# The Path Forward: Practices for Transcendence

PRACTICE: *See everyone you meet as a soul instead of just seeing their physical bodies.*

We're frequently attracted to romantic partners by the way someone looks, but Goddess Kalaratri's presence in our crown chakra inspires us to see beyond that. When you practice seeing everyone you meet in your life as a spiritual being versus just a body (that you may judge based on how it appears), you have an opportunity for deeper connections with others.

Seeing everyone as a soul also changes how you look at those who behave badly because you can recognize that we are all souls on our own journeys, progressing at different rates based on how ready we are for spiritual transformation and evolution. Recognizing the soul dimension of a person, above all else, means seeing what is common between you and all others: the essence of being.

This practice is also extremely beneficial if you struggle with attachments to the physical presence of other beings, humans as well as animals (like beloved pets). When you practice looking into their eyes and seeing them as eternal souls on a long journey back to their spiritual home, it helps to gain perspective. Because the soul in you and in others is the same, the more you connect with what is eternal within you, the more you can know that you are always connected with anyone you love at a spiritual level. Bonds that involve consideration of others' souls can never be broken, because the soul is eternal and infinite and lives beyond the lifetime of the body per ancient spiritual wisdom.

> The soul is eternal and infinite and lives beyond the lifetime of the body.

**PRACTICE:** *Repeat the mantra "I am not my body" to go beyond identifying with your physical being.*

In the ancient Vedic spiritual tradition, pleasure is one of the four goals of life. There is nothing wrong with enjoying the pleasures of radiant health, beautiful clothing, great sex, good food, and good company. In fact, the ancient spiritual wisdom of the Vedas says renunciation (the insignia of spiritual evolution) is not about abstaining from worldly objects and beings. It does not even necessarily mean lessening your possessions and enjoyment. You can be amongst all this, enjoying the pleasures of the body, while remaining on the spiritual path of renunciation.

Real renunciation means setting the right value for everything the world offers, to understand it as being fleeting and of trivial importance, even while being amongst it all and enjoying worldly pleasures. The problem with worldly pleasures is when you are obsessed by *desires* for them and start to identify yourself with these desires. This happens when you have food-related disorders (especially overeating and getting consumed by food cravings), sexual addictions, and a relentless pursuit of physical perfection (when you feel you are worthy only if you have large breasts or muscles, for example). Even restricting your food intake (in the case of anorexia) is still identifying with your body, by your desire to make it thin and excessively control what you take in.

However, when you see the body from a spiritual perspective, recognizing its limitations and potential to cause you to suffer, and you maintain proper control over your senses, you are not a sensualist even if you were to enjoy sensual things.

As someone who struggled with anorexia for much of my young life, I identified with the appearance of and control I exercised over my body. My suffering was all about the body. By adopting the mantra "I am not my body," I was able to shift my focus from my physical being to the part of me that goes beyond my body—my soul. That felt so liberating. I could then gradually begin to see my body more objectively. The more objectively I viewed my body (and the less I identified with it), the more I could care for it, by feeding myself healthy foods and practicing much of what I share in the first section of this book. With intention and care, I began to heal.

## PRACTICE: *Repeat the mantra "I am a soul" to strengthen your spiritual power.*

One of the things I love most about the Vedic spiritual tradition ways is that, while it acknowledges the many challenges of human life, it does not allow for us to be victims in any way, or to complain about our circumstances.

Rather, in this ancient tradition, we must reclaim our inner power, face challenges, and resolve them with faith in our hearts. Affirming that "I am a soul" helps to rise above fear, anger, and, in some cases, the shame that can manifest in the face of challenges. Though we may not have necessarily created the outer situations (in this lifetime), the more we take responsibility for the fact that something negative is happening, while remembering our power as a soul in the face of the obstacle(s), the more we will be able to rise to the challenges that present themselves in our lives.

You can call upon Goddess Kalaratri for support in this powerful practice of continually remembering and mentally asserting your power as a soul in the face of all difficulties. Imagine you are empowered with her weapons, and you too, as a soul, can exhale fierce fire from your nostrils to destroy armies of demons (an interesting way to see your challenges)!

## PRACTICE: *Work from fulfillment instead of for fulfillment.*

When you equate your sense of abundance with what the world gives you in terms of name, fame, money, and other material resources, you get lost in the pursuit of fulfillment from something outside yourself.

You can shift your focus from seeking the fulfillment the world has to offer to working from a place where you already feel happy and fulfilled no matter your circumstances. This is what it means to really put your heart into your work versus seeking emotional fulfillment from what you do. If you have a spiritual practice that helps you feel connected to the deepest parts of yourself already, then engage in it more often prior to beginning your professional or other type of work, so you can translate the kind of fulfillment you feel from these into your work. You can also refer to any of the practices in chapters 1, 2, and 4 for spiritual practices you can do to connect with your inner contentment.

It also helps to write in a journal where and how you feel stuck in terms of seeking fulfillment from your work. Do you sit and worry about achieving a certain goal (e.g., getting a promotion, having a certain number of followers, earning a specific amount of money)? Ask Goddess Kalaratri in your crown chakra to reveal to you first what kinds of outcomes you get consumed with desires for. Then, write affirmations of how your worth as a person is not linked to achieving those outcomes, and that you are worthy, no matter what, because you are a soul, first and foremost. This will empower you to move out of your attachment to outcomes.

Next, consider what kinds of actions lead you to achieve the outcomes you feel drawn to achieve. There is nothing wrong with acquisition, but it should never come from a space where your present happiness is dependent on future acquisition. If you are not happy with what you have now, you will never be happy with what you have in the future.

Finally, practice working from fulfillment by shifting your focus from the outcomes to the actions you can take toward achieving your goals. In the Bhagavad Gita, it is said that "you have a right to your actions only, never to the fruit of the actions." The more you start to find fulfillment in the actions themselves, while training your mind to stop fixating on an outcome from action, the more peace and prosperity you experience.

Prosperity follows a calm, peaceful mind that can plan an appropriate course of action and then stick to that course of action consistently.

**PRACTICE: *Stay fully present in the moment, without visiting the past or going into the future.***

A key part of spiritual healing is learning to live in the present moment without worrying about the past or developing anxiety for the future. According to the ancient wisdom of the Bhagavad Gita, perfect action should generate energy for you and should not dissipate it. The three factors that dissipate energy are attachment, hope, and fever.

Attachments are always related to the past. Dwelling on events and people from your past dissipates your energy. Hope, which normally has positive connotations, also has a flip side in the sense that it's related to the future and can bring anxiety over whether future events will occur. For example, if you really hope to get married or get a promotion, it's not wrong to have such aspirations, but when the hope gets too strong, it can lead to anxiety and obsession over these future events. Fever is getting too excited by the present moment, to the point of experiencing fear of loss (in the future) or generating desires for more of whatever is causing your excitement. Desire is the main cause of agitation and suffering in the mind, and being fully present means being free of desires.

The main feature of living fully in the present is action. The more you act, the more energy you gain. The main way you dissipate your energy is by being inactive. The highest form of activity, in this sense, is fighting and being a warrior, which Goddess Kalaratri models for us in our crown chakra.

**PRACTICE: *Do something daily that aligns with your core values.***

The best way to gain energy and power in your actions is by connecting them with a higher ideal that aligns with your core values. A higher ideal is something that goes beyond the small sphere of yourself and your family. Your ideal can extend to your community, country, and even all of humanity. The highest ideal possible is one that extends not just to human beings but to all living beings.

Gratitude is the parent of all other virtues. In ancient Indian spiritual scriptures, there is a practice of five *yajnas*, which are daily ways to express gratitude. The daily aspect of this practice underscores the need for consistency to yield the greatest power in what we do, like the way in which water flowing in one direction generates a force field.

Even though many of our ancestors made mistakes, it is still important to honor them in our hearts, as they gave us the gift of human birth. To be born human is the highest possible birth because it gives us the opportunity to evolve and to complete the entire cycle of birth and death, so our souls can be liberated. If you have living ancestors, pray for them. Depending on your situation, you can also send a card, visit, or help them. I feel a lot of gratitude toward my parents and am so happy I have always kept in touch with them, visited them, and cared for them when they were unwell.

We all receive much from Mother Earth. She gifts us the bounty of nature, food, trees, air, and sunshine. We can give back to Mother Nature by recycling, planting trees, caring for plants, composting, supporting threatened animals, and donating to organizations uplifting the well-being of the planet.

The daily action of serving mankind means seeing if there is a way you can support *any* person who is truly in need and who has no other way of having what you may gift them (like a warm meal for a person experiencing homelessness).

If you are fortunate to have found a spiritual teacher, then service offered to this soul is beneficial for expressing gratitude and deepening your knowledge.

Finally, even thinking of connecting with the goddesses is a way to express gratitude for the presence of divine beings. Lighting a candle every morning in honor of divinity and doing any of the other goddess-power-evoking practices are ways to give back to the divine, which blesses you with awakened consciousness in your crown chakra.

### PRACTICE: *Listen deeply to spiritual knowledge from any tradition that inspires you.*

The ancient Vedic spiritual tradition, like many old wisdom traditions, is an oral one. It is meant to be heard. Along with feeling our feelings (a necessary component of deep emotional healing), we need continual exposure to spiritual knowledge as profound food for our soul. Listening to wisdom from masters is an excellent way to absorb knowledge. This is because sound is the subtlest and most pervasive sense.

All oral traditions require deep listening to allow the knowledge to go deep into the recesses of our psyche. When you struggle with negativity in the face of challenges, it really helps to listen to someone else's positivity to receive inspiration and the strength to face what you need to face. Every morning, I listen to audio teachings of Swami Parthasarathy, an awakened soul who teaches ancient spiritual texts like the Bhagavad Gita verse by verse. He once shared that, at age ninety-three, he listens to these audio recordings himself simply to keep his mind absorbed in the highest truths.

It doesn't matter how long you listen, just that you do so on a daily basis, as consistency is the key to your progress spiritually. Sometimes I listen to spiritual lectures for more than an hour (if I have the time), and other times I do for as little as nine minutes. But I make it a point to keep up with it.

The ability to listen deeply to spiritual knowledge that awakens your highest consciousness is a gift from Goddess Kalaratri within your crown chakra.

**PRACTICE:** *Write spiritual truths over and over in a journal to reinforce them.*

In the ancient Vedic spiritual tradition, there is a two-step process for integrating what you have learned and making it your own. When you listen deeply to spiritual masters, you engage in the first step of this process, which is about hearing wisdom. This step is akin to eating spiritual food for your soul's evolution. You have to eat to take care of your physical body, just like you have to listen to the truth to care for your soul's health, growth, and evolution. The next step in the process is to contemplate what you have heard. This is like the process of digesting the food you eat. You have to digest the truths you listen to in order to be able to apply them to your everyday life.

One of the best ways to digest a particular teaching or a set of teachings that really resonates with you is to write it down, continually. This practice helps you stay present in the moment through action and reinforces the truth(s) for you, which helps you recall it at the appropriate moment, when you need to remember it. You can also write a mantra over and over again, a spiritual practice called *likhita japa*, which is similar to the japa mala, except that instead of using beads you use the written word.

**PRACTICE:** *Write reflections on illusions you face in your life and why they are not true.*

The practice of writing and reflecting on the different illusions you have unconsciously subscribed to and expressing, for yourself, why they are not true is an extremely potent way to evoke Goddess Kalaratri's illusion-blasting force in your crown chakra. So many modern personal transformation programs include journaling as a primary tool for facilitating healing and growth. There is something to this.

The hands are a very important seat of karma (positive or negative) in ancient wisdom traditions. When you use your hands to see through your own illusions, you really evoke the power of Goddess Kalaratri within you. The kind of strength and courage you will gain in the face of illusions will magnify exponentially. The hands give you the power to manifest your visions, intentions, and quest to realize your divine Self.

One interesting journal prompt is to write about when you have truly loved others and when you have been attached, so you can see and feel the difference for yourself. You can also do the same exercise by reflecting on when you have felt truly loved by someone and when you have just been on the receiving end of someone's attachments. Attachment comes with invisible threads of selfishness, or a desire to manipulate or control another so we can feel secure. Love blossoms by your identification with others and becoming one with another.

When it comes to this kind of deep burning away of long-held illusions, you have the power to dramatically propel the course of your personal spiritual evolution—something you need to strive and struggle for by yourself. You may receive guidance from sages, but you have to make an effort for your own spiritual growth. No one can do it for you. Only you can save yourself. As the wisdom of the Bhagavad Gita reveals: "You must raise yourself by yourself." You must work through your own illusions to find your true, divine Self, be devoted to this Self, and contemplate the Self throughout your life. Spiritual practice is a full-time awareness of what is eternal in your life. It is not a part-time ritualized practice only.

What you do to progress this way spiritually also remains with you eternally. Knowledge is the one thing that can never be taken away. When you live by knowledge, you experience the tremendous power of the practice of aligning yourself to Goddess Kalaratri, the transcendent power of divinity within you.

# Chapter 8

# Embracing New Beginnings

*I am the Self, seated in the heart of all beings; I am the beginning, the*
*middle and also the end of all beings . . .*

*. . . I am Ananta of Nagas (snakes) . . . of beasts I am the lion . . .*
*Of seasons, I am the flowery season (spring) . . . I am victory, I am*
*determination, I am sattva (purity) of the sattvika (pure).*

*. . . And also I am that which is the seed of all beings, O Arjuna.*

—BHAGAVAD GITA, chapter 10, verses 20–39

## Cultivating Rejuvenation

After the illusion-blasting intensity of the battles to achieve strong
boundaries and transcendence in chapters 6 and 7, we are now blessed
by a beautiful new beginning in chapter 8. This new beginning is the one
bestowed upon us by the power of the knowledge we have converted into
our own inner wisdom.

Day 8 to me is a day for fresh starts—and a whole lot of fun! Just as
there are similarities between the powers of transformation and transcendence on days 3 and 7, I find similarities between the power of love
from day 4 and the power of rejuvenation that we cultivate on day 8.

I always look forward to day 8 because it is a day when we give ourselves the opportunity for pure enjoyment of life's pleasures. At this stage in the spiritual journey of Navratri, having released our attachments to the body in chapter 7, we can create a new reality–one in which we can truly enjoy the pleasures of life because we are not full of cravings or desires. The self-control we cultivate in chapter 2 serves as the foundation for the pure enjoyment we experience in chapter 8. Controlling your mind at this stage, however, does not necessarily mean restricting the quantity of your enjoyment.

In the Vedas, Sage Durvasa eats food freely–and constantly–and yet is known as one who is on an eternal fast. Lord Krishna was known to have spent time with many milkmaids yet is also legendary for being an eternal *brahmachari* (celibate). What reconciles these apparent contradictions is the value that we ascribe to the pleasures of the senses. Possession and enjoyment do not define your renunciation. Real renunciation means being able to set the correct value for all the pleasures the world has to offer and to see them as transient and ephemeral, even as you are enjoying them.

I found myself applying this understanding of true renunciation to romantic relationships in New York during the COVID-19 pandemic of 2020–2021. Even though I had been living my Navratri practice for almost a decade, I still found (and continue to discover) opportunities for new beginnings, and during this strange and unprecedented time, I began to approach love differently. I started getting to know several men I had met online, treating them all equally, while focusing on my own emotional needs, so I could discern who could truly love me, like Radha loves Krishna.

Cultivating the power of rejuvenation also meant recommitting to my own healing. Once I felt settled in my new home and my new professional role, I opened myself up to receiving love, healing, encouragement, and guidance from all kinds of healers. Doing so empowered me to hone my own discernment when it came to the new relationships I was forming and ensured I did not repeat old behavioral patterns as part of my new approach to love.

In addition, cultivating the power of rejuvenation allowed me to focus on how I inhabit my physical body. With the fearlessness Goddess Kalaratri helped me develop, I embraced food, fashion, and fitness, three things I had largely neglected in the past, in a whole new way. I aimed to feel good in my own skin, without wanting my body to be any specific way.

One of the meanings of my name, Ananta, is "the king of the Naga serpents." The cobra is a powerful symbol of shedding the old skin and growing thick new skin. As my old skin literally peeled off my face with chemical peels (which, despite what its name suggests, is an all-natural ancient Egyptian skin treatment), I felt a similar shedding process take place with respect to my old beliefs that I was not worthy or lovable. I relinquished my need to hide out of fear and shame. I embraced being on camera and became visible to the world online.

In this chapter, we will get to know the beautiful Goddess Maha Gauri, an eight-year-old girl who blesses us with the innocence and youthfulness that flower with wisdom. We'll also learn how to activate the power of play to rejuvenate ourselves on all levels—body, mind, and intellect— and to fully embrace the present moment.

## Knowing MAHA GAURI

After killing off so many demons in her terrifying form as Kalaratri, Goddess Durga is left with navy-blue skin, which has been burned to ashes from the heat and intensity of her battles with demons. She goes to Lord Brahma, asking for her skin to be transformed and brightened after the battles she fought and won.

Lord Brahma gives his blessing for her to bathe in Mansarovar in the Himalayas. Her battle-scarred skin peels off, revealing fresh new skin

that glows, for which she becomes known as "Maha Gauri," the great, shining one. Not only is her skin new in this moment, but Goddess Durga also appears as an eight-year-old girl. She is reunited again with Lord Shiva, whose trident and drum (representing primordial sound vibrations) she carries in her hands. As she did in her first incarnation as Goddess Shailputri, Durga as Maha Gauri rides a white bull.

Goddess Maha Gauri represents the power of rejuvenation, purity, and inner beauty that you connect with when you face the battles of your life with resolve, strength, and clarity. The fact that she rides a white bull and holds a trident (like Durga's avatar as Shailputri in chapter 1 does) demonstrates how the eighth step of the Navratri spiritual journey is one of new beginnings. We are blessed with new beginnings through the power of our perseverance toward detachment and disciplined practices to overcome our own inner demons of illusions.

Your skin is considered a mirror for your mind according to the ancient healing wisdom of Ayurveda. Goddess Maha Gauri is an emblem for the true beauty that comes from digging deep to resolve challenges in your life and finding your real spiritual power, which confers lasting youth, vitality, and a glow that truly comes from within.

As someone who noticed how much my own skin broke out as I faced the long-held illusions I had, it was a blessing to learn about the ancient Egyptian practice of chemical peels, which Queen Cleopatra once famously used for her own skin. As I went through a series of these peels, I always found strength from the story of Goddess Maha Gauri, who transformed her own adversity by literally peeling away the old skin and growing thicker, brighter skin.

## Taking Inventory

How do you know you are growing spiritually at this stage of the Navratri spiritual journey? You know by how much you experience something

# REJUVENATION & THE EIGHTH CHAKRA

The power of rejuvenation is connected with your eighth chakra (known as the higher heart chakra). It is said to be located above your crown chakra (just about at the top of your head). The kind of rejuvenation we experience in the eighth chakra is of a special kind, because it follows the enlightenment that starts to dawn upon us in the seventh (crown) chakra. There is a rebirth that comes from facing the truths that the seventh chakra puts us in touch with.

Maha Gauri is depicted in a way that is similar to the way Catholics portray Mother Mary. This goddess is depicted as an eight-year-old child. She holds a trident (a symbol of new beginnings) and a drum, both of which are connected to Lord Shiva. Her youthfulness, compassion, love, and innocence are symbolic of the vitality and rejuvenation we gain from undergoing intense spiritual disciplines designed to reunite us with Lord Shiva (our highest consciousness) within our own being.

called *ascharya*, which means "wonderment" in Sanskrit. It is a child-like innocence and curiosity at the great mystery, marvel, and majesty of God, the goddesses, or however you choose to acknowledge the higher consciousness that connects us all.

Your higher Self is one with God. It is omnipotent, omnipresent, and omniscient. Transcendent. And infinite. You cannot perceive the Self with your senses. Neither can your mind feel it via your emotions. Your intellect cannot conceive it. That which lies beyond your body, mind, and intellect is a wonder. It is ascharya.

Have you ever . . .

- Experienced the wonder of nature in all her majesty?

- Witnessed events in your life that seemed like miracles, which took you beyond your mundane worldly existence and gave you a taste of something truly sublime?

- Noticed how synchronistic the weaving together of your own life is when you surrender to simply observing without trying to control it?

- Had events that seemed like total catastrophes end up becoming the biggest blessings in disguise in your life?

- Contemplated how magical it is that leaves change colors, fall off trees, and then come back again when it is their time?

This is all ascharya. A divine wonderment. Ascharya is such a beautiful concept that it is quoted in the Bhagavad Gita, chapter 2, verse 29 from chapter 1, section ii, verse 7 of the Upanishads (in Kathopanishad): "One sees This [Self] as a wonder so also another speaks of This as a wonder, another hears of This as a wonder; and though having heard, none knows This at all."

As you advance on your spiritual journey, you will experience wonderment more and more. The more you know, the less you feel you know, and the more wonderment you will have. As you evolve spiritually, you will no longer need miracles to see the divinity as ever present. The sight of a sunrise or sunset will eventually move you to wonderment.

As you continue growing, even a mere flower or fruit can move you, as it did for William Wordsworth in his beautiful poem "I Wandered Lonely as a Cloud":

And then my heart with pleasure fills,

And dances with the daffodils.

# Embracing New Beginnings

*Release the past by seeing those who have hurt you as lost children who did not know better.*

In the Bhagavad Gita, Lord Krishna uses the word *balaha* a lot. *Balaha* means "child" in Sanskrit. You know you have evolved to a higher level on your spiritual journey when you can see the bullies, predators, and even social media trolls in your life as balaha, or children who did not know any better, much in the way Jesus once said, "Forgive them, Father, for they know not what they do."

When my anger released itself through my skin, I realized that I was still longing for love from all the people who had hurt me in the past. At that point, I recognized that people who had hurt me did so because they did not have the capacity to love me. That mindset shift allowed me to stop wanting or expecting them to correct their behaviors. I genuinely saw the helpless child in all those who had hurt me in the past, and it freed me to move forward with my life, without wanting any kind of explanation or apology from any of them.

I realized it was my responsibility to love myself more fully and deeply than I ever had before in my life. As an empath, I was programmed by my nature, childhood conditioning, and societal conditioning as a woman to always put the needs of others ahead of my own. Undoing these behavioral patterns would be challenging, but also imperative. Once I saw these truths, I began to truly value and honor my own needs and feelings in a new way.

*Receive the support you have exclusively given to others in the past.*

Being able to receive is something that does not come easily to many of us, but it is necessary to maintain the cycle of giving and receiving, learning and teaching, and flowing without burnout. Selflessness without self-care, after all, is a recipe for burnout.

Ten years into this journey, my discernment, which was much more developed at this point, allowed me to see clearly who could offer me love and who could not. As a result, I started investing more time in connecting with those who could care for me. Every time I resisted the idea of spending money on myself to speak with healers of various modalities, my higher Self overrode that self-sabotaging inner ego voice and did it anyway. Every dollar I spent on myself was energy I invested in loving myself and caring for my needs.

It was very helpful to have multiple people to reach out to at any given moment when I needed something. Connecting with various healers ensured I never got too dependent upon any one person. It also bolstered my confidence. Now I know that if I have a problem, I also have the strength to overcome it by asking for help and by working through my karma so it need not keep recurring.

*Tune in to your body to see what messages it has for you, and then lovingly respond to each one.*

The body is always communicating with us. It is up to us to listen deeply to what it wishes to express. I realized, as my skin continued breaking out despite all the treatments, that it had very important messages to convey to me.

My skin wanted me to stop hiding out of fear of being rejected, attacked, shamed, or judged. It wanted me to stop saying things that did not align with my true Self for the sake of others' approval and acceptance. It wanted me to stop keeping secrets. My skin also wanted to make me deeply understand that anything I looked to others for (like love, acceptance, protection, and support) I could and should first cultivate within myself. It also wanted me to know that anyone can leave me but that I will never leave or abandon myself. Only then, it said, would it not have to keep erupting to continuously remind me of these messages.

*Let go of clothing and items that remind you of painful experiences, and consider what new clothing, items, and experiences you invite into your heart and life.*

Every item we own carries energy. When we are awake to this fact, it becomes imperative that we act upon it, let go of the old, and invite new beginnings into our lives. I went through my belongings and screened each and every item to see if it carried energy of my past relationships and experiences that I no longer needed.

As I considered what new clothing, items, and experiences I would invite into my life, it was important to me that each new thing I brought into my home would hold deep symbolic value, that each would somehow serve to remind me of my true Self. As I chose new clothing, I avoided the color black, as it is said to evoke the quality of *tamas*, or mental inertia and darkness in Ayurveda and Yoga psychology. I have no aversion to darkness as such (it's where our deepest treasures of wisdom are ultimately discovered, after all), but I chose to cultivate more *sattva* (mental clarity, purity, and peace) by wearing softer pastel colors that remind me of the rising sun (a symbol of the soul in the Vedas). I chose to place beautiful statues of Goddess Lakshmi, Goddess Saraswati, and Lord Ganesha (the elephant-headed remover of obstacles, who also gives us obstacles to remind us of our true nature) on my desk altar. The same deities I had puzzled over seeing in Hindu temples, I embraced for how they reminded me of the battles I had fought–and won–to stay true to my higher Self.

It felt very healing to embrace the rejuvenating spiritual power of flowers. I bought a painting of lotus flowers, as they are not only a weapon in the hands of Goddess Maha Gauri (and many other Navratri goddesses) but also symbolic of eternity, purity, and rebirth. Just as a lotus grows in mud, pure beauty can emerge from the dirt of obstacles in our lives, when we cultivate and grow the seed of knowledge. I also bought and grew a beautiful tropical hibiscus plant in the heart of New York City. I still wonder how it blossomed all through the years of the pandemic. Hibiscus is said to be the favorite flower of Goddess Durga. I grew aloe vera, a rejuvenating herb that is known as a woman's best friend in Ayurveda. It benefits every aspect of women's health, cools the body, and supports the release of toxic buildup from trauma.

After embracing new experiences through the sense of sight and scent with flowers, I also created a whole new relationship with food. Though I have never tired of cooking and eating the same Ayurvedic recipes during the past decade, during the pandemic, I received an overwhelming number of requests for healthier Ayurvedic versions of people's favorite foods. I began to create Ayurvedic versions of popular foods like pizzas, pastas, Thai food, and Indian curries. For my own part, having begun my martial arts training, I observed how much hungrier I felt.

I had no idea how much I would enjoy the cooking process! I loved procuring a blender (something I had never had), operating an oven (something I never did), and buying new ingredients to cook with, like fresh coconut milk (not the canned kind). The aromas in my kitchen were magical. Like Sage Durvasa, I enjoyed a wide variety of food freely, without getting caught up by the desire for anything in particular. Though I had not suffered from food cravings since 2011 when I committed to an Ayurvedic diet, I had spent ten years eating a very monotonous diet, which made this phase in my culinary journey a revelation. Every day was a new feast, and I enjoyed it all because I ate only what I discerned was beneficial for my body's particular needs according to Ayurveda.

I found such great unexpected joy in the new dishes I created that I began to share them with the world, and I embraced being visible online. It did not come from a desire for recognition or approval, but simply from a place of feeling that it was what I ought to do as a way to share what I had learned about holistic health during a time when the world was in dire need of it.

In addition to sharing what I had learned about cooking because it felt like the right thing to do, I also started choosing clothes because they made me feel good. I picked colorful garments that flattered my body and reflected who I am, instead of choosing clothes that helped me hide out of shame, as I had previously done. In Ayurveda, beauty is an expression of purity, balance, and harmony (the mental quality of *sattva*, a word whose root is *sat*, meaning "Truth"). In the Vedas, we have an expression *Satyam Shivam Sundaram*. It means Truth is God—and also means pure beauty. Not the kind of beauty that comes from a place of competitive feelings, or from artificial, harsh chemicals that damage your body, or that uses excessive makeup, fake eyelashes, or hair extensions with the intention to seduce a man or woman to be your lover. This is the beauty that reflects clarity, which is all-natural, wholesome, and most of all, pure.

### Start fresh in romantic relationships.

In the Vedas, deities are balanced in terms of having both masculine and feminine attributes, as God and consciousness ultimately transcend gender. Goddess Durga herself is both fierce (a traditionally masculine attribute) and compassionate (a traditionally feminine quality). In the process of being online to share the wisdom I learned, I attracted a lot of romantic attention from men. This time, with the greater strength and security I felt in my body from my martial arts training, and having transcended my shame around my body from childhood conditioning, I was more connected with the masculine side of myself. In accepting both masculine and feminine attributes in myself, I found myself feeling more integrated, balanced, and comfortable with masculine energy in male-identifying bodies.

I set a new intention that, instead of replaying the role of the goddess Radha by becoming devoted to a Lord Krishna type of man (surrounded by women), I would find balance in relationships by being like Krishna. Lord Krishna plays the flute and is playful and eternally youthful. He loves everyone, shares his wisdom as a spiritual teacher, and has many wives, but has a special place in his heart for Goddess Radha, who loves him purely, with devotion. And though he is surrounded by women, he is still known as an eternal brahmachari, who follows Goddess Brahmacharini's protocol of brahmacharya.

This is because he is not attached to sensual pleasures. He fully sees their ephemeral nature even while enjoying them, and he also remains full of joy, beauty, lightness, and playfulness even while bringing profound wisdom to the world. He embodies the power of rejuvenation in this way. I love that the name Ananta is androgynous, given to both men and women. Bringing together the pair of opposites inherent in male and female genders, I began my journey of embodying the essence of Lord Krishna to connect with Goddess Maha Gauri's power of rejuvenation in romantic relationships.

A full decade after I began applying Ayurveda's holistic wisdom, I feel much healthier and stronger than I have ever felt before. I know this youthfulness is not only due to my physical health but also to all the spiritual baggage I've let go of. Spiritual practice is the ultimate rejuvenation. Because of this, I do not feel the pressure of a biological clock ticking to cause me to want to get married quickly, and instead I've been able to focus on being playful and having fun in relationships with multiple men, while always honoring my own self-chosen, self-respecting boundaries. This has allowed me the safety to enjoy and learn from each experience, without focusing exclusively on one person as the answer to all my prayers, until I find someone who is as devoted to me as Radha is to Krishna.

This detached approach to dating has brought me a newfound sense of fun and freedom in an area of my life that I once only associated with pain and shame. It also provides me the opportunity to practice discernment in terms of whom to give my time. By giving myself all the love, care, fun, attention, validation, protection, honesty, and enjoyment I once unconsciously wanted from a partner (and behaved codependently to try to get), I treat myself like a queen. I only keep men around me (in work and in romance) who honor and respect me, because that is what I retrained myself to become familiar with. This prevents me from re-creating my part in old relationship dynamics in new relationships.

Practicing letting go of desires in love has been extremely empowering. Being able to relax, surrender, and have a strong foundation of radiant health (including a predictable menstrual cycle) are the keys to natural fertility and conception in Ayurveda. Being open to marriage and having children, if they come organically to me (but not at all desperate for either of these), helps me simply practice being fully present to each moment, like a child is. When I need to cry, I cry. Mostly, however, with the knowledge of what is eternal versus ephemeral ingrained deep within me, I find myself staying lighthearted even amidst very intense situations that arise while dating, and thereby enjoying everything that comes and goes with a newfound sense of wonderment.

# The Path Forward: Practices for Rejuvenation

**PRACTICE:** *Practice Cobra Pose with the intention of connecting with the spirit of rebirth it represents.*

The cobra is a deity in its own right in the Vedic spiritual tradition, said to have many lives. It is representative of power. It also represents fertility, rebirth, and protection. When the snake is hungry and finds no food, it simply eats its own tail and then grows another.

The snake is so strong because it is basically one long muscle. Learning martial arts as part of my process of shedding all the emotional baggage of my time of spiritual study, and regaining my strength, was so empowering. Within just a few months, my muscles became the strongest they've ever been, and that strength really helps me embody the spirit of the serpent I am named after.

When you practice Cobra Pose, it helps to connect with its survivor spirit, against all odds. To practice the pose, lie on your abdomen with your hands underneath your shoulders. Lift your head, neck, shoulders, and chest up off the ground. Pull yourself up from the base of your spine. Close your eyes and imagine yourself to be as powerful and strong as a thousand-headed cobra as you rise free from any emotional baggage weighing you down.

**PRACTICE:** *Do something fun that frees your inner child.*

Goddess Maha Gauri is depicted as a young girl. When you want to awaken your eighth chakra, after the intensity of having your illusions dismantled by Goddess Kalaratri in the seventh chakra, and the whole purification process that ensued in the previous chakras, it helps to have some fun. The fun you will have at this stage of the spiritual journey will be of a different kind than what you may have found fun before. It will be a new kind of fun, one that is truly innocent and childlike.

Do you love to sing in the shower? Go for long car rides in beautiful natural surroundings? Watch *Saturday Night Live*? Play board games or sports? Give yourself permission to enjoy yourself, as a way to rejuvenate your spirit and leave you feeling connected with the spirit of the youthful Goddess Maha Gauri within you.

## PRACTICE: *Apply aloe vera gel to your skin to rejuvenate your physical body.*

Aloe vera is known in the ancient healing wisdom of Ayurveda as "that which keeps you eternally youthful," like Goddess Maha Gauri. This common but incredibly beneficial herb supports your skin, digestion, and hair and reduces inflammation and any external burns or burning sensations you may feel on your skin.

There is some heat and intensity involved in the spiritual journey, as you start to pierce the veil of your illusions (in the seventh chakra). That is because seeing through illusions in your life can trigger the heat of anger. When I recognized all the ways that the trauma I experienced as an adult mirrored what I went through in childhood, the suppressed anger I felt came out through heat and breakouts in my skin.

The cooling, soothing quality of aloe vera was extremely beneficial to my skin to manage the heat. You can use aloe vera if you suffer from breakouts or have hot skin—just apply the gel directly to the irritated places, by itself or with honey and turmeric. You can take up to two teaspoons of aloe vera gel to relieve constipation. You can also apply this wonderful gel to your hair to help prevent hair loss (which can occur when you have too much heat in your body). You can drink an eighth of a cup of fresh aloe vera juice two or three times until your fever subsides and your appetite returns in cases of feverish symptoms. It's also helpful to gently put some aloe vera gel onto your eyelids if you have pain in your eyes and need to rejuvenate yourself from too much computer usage.

## PRACTICE: *Shed old clothes and replace them with fresh new clothing.*

The eighth day of Navratri, when Goddess Maha Gauri is worshipped, is a day for new beginnings at all levels, even in terms of your clothing. Followers of Navratri typically don fresh new clothing on this special day.

As I continued to heal, to rejuvenate, and to acclimate to my new life, I slowly yet steadily changed almost every piece of clothing I owned. I made sure to choose what made me feel good in my own skin. It was so therapeutic and liberating in ways that go beyond skin deep.

When you examine your wardrobe, evaluate every piece of clothing you have for what sentimental value you have attached to it. Does a shirt remind you of someone you need to let go of your attachment to? Are there any pieces of clothing you own that you no longer really connect with, or that don't fit you, or otherwise make you feel a little off? It will be so liberating to donate them to someone who can really benefit from them and slowly gift yourself brand-new clothes, to reflect the purity of Goddess Maha Gauri within you.

## PRACTICE: *Have a spontaneous dance party.*

Dancing is a way to express the pure, childlike spirit of the goddess in your eighth chakra. In India, all the classical dance forms are artistic depictions of the mythological stories in this book, and so much other ancient spiritual folklore. There were women in ancient India who actually married temples and dedicated their entire lives to dance as a profound spiritual practice of uniting with the divinity within.

When you have a victory in your life, it's important to celebrate! There are so many small victories we have in our everyday lives that no one else will ever see but that matter to us. You can express the joy of your private victories by dancing to your favorite music, all by yourself or with a beloved friend, child, or pet.

## PRACTICE: *Do something new that brings you pleasure and well-being.*

Goddess Maha Gauri represents the new beginnings you experience with the dawning of higher knowledge and awareness. You can remember her within you whenever you do something new that brings you a sense of enjoyment and well-being.

I personally was never a big fan of cooking as I feared I would end up as a housewife and mom who cooks all the time and whose presence always gets taken for granted. Once I saw that I would need to cook to meet the requests of students, clients, editors, friends, and social media followers for new recipes, it changed everything for me.

By connecting with the intention of being of service to many people and families so that they could take their health into their own hands, I started to feel empowered and free with the very thing I had feared would resign me to a life of limited freedoms. And I was so pleasantly surprised at how much I then started to find pleasure, well-being, and a whole lot of fun in every aspect of this new activity! From researching and gathering ingredients to learning new things about foods to chopping and creating custom seasonal spice blends to expanding beyond stovetop recipes to using a blender and oven for the first time and even getting really into food photography, the whole process became a new kind of fun for me.

You can expand your pleasure and well-being vis-à-vis seasonal Ayurveda food by checking out my website for recipes (theancientway .co/blog) if you feel so inspired. Other ideas for new activities that bring you both pleasure and well-being:

- A new style of exercise (e.g., Tai Chi, Qigong, Yoga, biking, Pilates, boxing, martial arts)
- Dance (of any kind)
- Learning a musical instrument (like piano, guitar, or flute)
- Reading interesting books about inspiring figures in history
- Taking a course to learn about holistic health (we offer several via my organization, The Ancient Way)
- Traveling to a new destination (even near you) where you can learn from the wisdom of the ancient ancestors of the place

As one of the three forms of Goddess Saraswati (the goddess of arts, creativity, wisdom, and higher learning), Maha Gauri will bless you in whatever new endeavor you choose to take on.

When contemplating what new activity you'd like to begin, ask yourself what you've always wanted to do but stopped yourself from doing. Is there something you're interested in because you see the benefits (like taking on a new exercise program or learning a new art form) but about which you feel some resistance? I found it helpful to explore my own resistance and then transform it through the power of intention, a practice we will go into much more in the next chapter.

## PRACTICE: *Approach boring experiences with a spirit of play.*

Every new day comes with opportunities for new beginnings when you approach life with a spirit of play, adventure, and personal growth. In the ancient Vedic wisdom, joy is not something that is derived from outside. It's something that comes from deep within. You, therefore, have the opportunity to make even the most mundane experiences of life fun–like dealing with daily traffic or even taking a shower!

You can infuse a sense of play into these experiences by creating a new soundtrack full of your favorite music to listen to during traffic or putting together your favorite comedic podcasts to hear on the way. You can approach showering as an exciting time to cleanse your whole being from the inside out and try infusing your shower with beautiful floral scents and petals that can help to invigorate your space.

Ultimately, changing your perspective toward something ordinary is what empowers you to move from a feeling of drudgery to one of inner joy that awakens within you the power of Goddess Maha Gauri.

### PRACTICE: *Plant seeds (of herbs, fruits, flowers, or trees).*

Mother Nature is full of abundant blessings. Every seed you plant, whether it be a fruit, a flower, or a tree, carries within it the power of long-lasting rejuvenation, not just for you but for all those who come into contact with it. When you plant something with the intention of growing a specific quality in your life in harmony with the plant's growth, it can be a truly beautiful and healing experience. The bountiful wisdom of Ayurveda tells us that some specific medicinal friends in nature can be beneficial to you for healing.

Coriander is one such friend. It is great for your physical and emotional heart, and it also boosts your digestion while simultaneously releasing heat from your body. After you grow it, you can add it as a garnish to your food for digestive support. You can also mix water with coriander leaves to make a paste to apply to your head for relief of heat-related headaches. You can also apply this paste to your skin to help give your skin a new beginning in terms of clearing up acne, rashes, and rosacea.

Planting a fig tree is another great idea. Figs support fertility, digestion, and natural beauty. Many people use them as a mild laxative. They also reenergize your body when you feel fatigue, exhaustion, overwhelm, low energy, and weakness, and they can reduce feelings of anxiety, burnout, and stress. You can also eat two figs per day to help you gain weight if needed or to simply improve your complexion.

Jasmine flowers are an amazing emblem of Goddess Maha Gauri, who is depicted in the white color this flower normally comes in. Growing jasmine flowers is beneficial because their scent is so pleasant at nighttime. When you have wounds, eczema, itching, burns, or any pain at all, you can also apply a paste made of eight to ten jasmine flowers to these areas to give you relief.

Beyond the benefits of all these fruits, flowers, and herbs, the greatest benefit of the practice of planting seeds is the rejuvenation and sense of new beginnings you experience in your eighth chakra when you start a beautiful and positive new activity.

### PRACTICE: *Start fresh in your relationships.*

It's important to try to bring Goddess Maha Gauri's innocence into the realm of relationships, where misunderstandings and mishaps can easily happen despite the best of intentions. This goes for all your relationships. Is there someone you haven't spoken to for a long time (like a friend or relative) you'd like to reconnect with? Or is there an argument you had with someone close to you about a trivial matter that you can let go of? So many disagreements we have with others can be resolved when someone practices letting go and when both parties agree to try again.

Starting fresh does not erase the mistakes of the past. Rather, it's an invitation to view those you are in relationships with through softer eyes, to forgive, and to demonstrate a willingness to begin again, without the baggage of the past. Starting fresh means being able to approach the same relationship from a new vantage point, one in which you can allow your heart and intuition (cultivated in earlier chapters) to guide you.

# Chapter 9

# Leading with Integrity

*Whatever a leader does, that alone other people do;*
*whatever standard a leader sets, the world follows.*

—BHAGAVAD GITA, chapter 3, verse 21

*Having renounced attachment to the fruit of action,*
*ever content, depending on nothing, one does not do*
*anything though one is engaged in action.*

—BHAGAVAD GITA, chapter 4, verse 20

## Cultivating Intentionality

After embracing new beginnings and ensuring we feel rejuvenated by independently meeting our needs, the ninth and final step of the nine-part Navratri spiritual practice is harnessing the power of intention so that we may live with integrity.

By this point in the cycle, we have undergone a journey that has brought us to a place where we can ethically lead others to discover their own wholeness and, therein, their potential. Through the power of intention, we continue to embody integrity in both senses of the word—moral uprightness and being undividedly whole.

It makes so much sense to me why selfless service, leading others, and giving back come as the ninth and final step of the Navratri spiritual journey. To be ready for this moment, we have to fortify ourselves with stability and self-control in order to undergo the fire of transformation, cultivate the power of loving our true Self, express ourselves with sound and silence, trust our intuition, set and maintain healthy boundaries, transcend honor and dishonor (and success and failure), and have a healthy enjoyment of pleasure in our lives. All this empowers us to lead in a pure way, one that does not inflate or deflate our ego. This is relevant for all types of leadership–whether you lead a company, a cause, or a family–but it is particularly important for spiritual leaders, gurus, and healers so that they can avoid the many pitfalls that occur when people seek to fulfill hidden desires in the name of spirituality.

When we talk about cultivating the power of intentionality, we are setting sacred intentions that extend beyond ourselves. At this advanced stage of the journey, we experience our true nature as spiritual beings by simply doing what we ought to do, as instruments, without desires or expectations that might taint our actions. In the Vedic spiritual tradition, we believe all living beings, including plants and animals, are reflections of one universal soul. To act in service of as many beings as we can acknowledges our divine interconnectedness.

In this chapter, you will meet Goddess Siddhidhatri, the bestower of *siddhis* (divine gifts), and learn to offer your gifts in service of as many beings as possible. Writing this book and creating my own organization was my personal way of expressing the power of Goddess Siddhidhatri within me, from a space of deep humility and gratitude that comes from knowing that all I have been given comes from God. Just as a lion is a great symbol of sovereignty, my mission in all that I do is to remain free from dependency, and to set those I serve free from dependency as well. So that we may all simply shine with the light of the radiant sun.

# Knowing SIDDHIDHATRI

In the beginning, when the universe was a huge void of emptiness, there was no light, no species, no time, no nature, and no creation of any kind. Suddenly, out of nowhere, a bright, celestial light shone all over the place. The light was full of divine power that illuminated every bit of the emptiness.

After a few moments, the light formed itself into a great creator goddess called Siddhidhatri, who then created the holy trinity of gods known as Brahma (the god of creation), Vishnu (the god of maintenance), and Shiva (the god of destruction). Siddhidhatri instructed each of these gods on their specific duties to the world and assigned them responsibilities that would enable them to fulfill their duties. The three gods obliged the goddess and followed their required spiritual practices.

Pleased with their dedication, Goddess Siddhidhatri blessed the trinity of deities abundantly with many supernatural divine powers. She also gifted each of them female consorts to support them in their respective roles of creation, maintenance, and destruction. Goddess Saraswati became the wife of Lord Brahma, to support all creation in the universe. Goddess Lakshmi became the wife of Lord Vishnu, to preserve all the goodness in the universe. Goddess Kali became the wife of Lord Shiva, to unleash the power of destruction of what is evil in the universe.

With her incredible fiery power, Goddess Siddhidhatri continued to create more gods, demons, demigods, galaxies, planets, the solar system, flora, fauna, land, animals, mountains, and everything else that exists today. All types of gifts and talents we have come from her. We must use our gifts wisely to complete our worship of Goddess Siddhidhatri for the ultimate, lasting happiness, peace, wisdom, and realization of our highest nature in life.

I love how the spiritual journey of the nine nights of Navratri culminates in the ninth goddess, Siddhidhatri, whose message to us is of the

importance of putting all our gifts and blessings to noble use for the benefit of as many as possible. When we are able to overcome our inner demons and fight outer demons from a place of keeping our inner peace intact, we may give back to others and complete our spiritual journey. Many people wonder if it is selfish to withdraw and go deeply inward on a spiritual path. But Siddhidhatri's presence at the end of the journey highlights how we are only able to give our greatest gifts in service of others when we do so from a place of integration and a feeling of wholeness and fullness that comes from undergoing a spiritual journey to know our true Self. Only by unveiling our true Self can we inspire others to do the same.

> Only by unveiling our true Self can we inspire others to do the same.

Goddess Siddhidhatri blesses us with a sense of responsibility for the divine gifts and talents with which we have been endowed. All the abilities we have come from a divine source. We are not meant to hoard them but to share them with as many as we can. In doing so, we will be blessed with a happiness that goes beyond the transient satisfaction we experience when our desires are fulfilled. The kind of happiness that Goddess Siddhidhatri blesses us with is a spiritual joy that goes beyond sorrow. This joy is your true nature. It is the gift and blessing of knowing your true Self.

## Taking Inventory

Just as the fire of transformation in chapter 3 required knowing whether you are operating more from your ego's power or from the power of your soul, so too is it is necessary to determine the same thing in order to lead with integrity.

# INTENTION & THE NINTH CHAKRA

The power of intention is connected with the ninth and final chakra (also known as an astral chakra, a subtle spiritual counterpart to your physical body). Its location is slightly above the crown of your head. Cultivating the power of intention is what you can do to kick-start your spiritual journey. Along the way, you will reevaluate and recommit yourself to that journey, to keep yourself motivated about what matters most to you.

Siddhidhatri is depicted as having supernatural healing powers. She has four arms and is surrounded by yogis, saints, gods, and devotees, whom she blesses with divine powers to be used for noble purposes. These divine powers come with an understanding of the responsibility that we must apply our gifts in service of our highest aims in life and in service of all beings. The spiritual journey of Navratri is about preparing to share with others from a place of having undergone personal transformation. This ensures that what we give to others comes from the deepest place within us, which blesses us as well as all those who receive what we have to offer. Everyone has a gift, and Siddhidhatri helps to clarify and ensure its heartfelt expression.

Determining whether you resonate more with your soul power or your ego power in each category below can help you identify in which areas you might like to set specific intentions so that you can be the best leader, parent, or teacher you can be.

| | ALWAYS | FREQUENTLY | SOMETIMES | INFREQUENTLY | NEVER |
|---|---|---|---|---|---|
| Do I find relative ease in my work and relationships, even when obstacles arise, due to feeling connected with a higher power? | 1 | 2 | 3 | 4 | 5 |
| Do I turn inward to discover the divine as my parent? | 1 | 2 | 3 | 4 | 5 |
| Am I realistic about my mistakes and shortcomings? | 1 | 2 | 3 | 4 | 5 |
| Do I refuse to compromise inner freedom and my values for outer abundance? | 1 | 2 | 3 | 4 | 5 |
| Do I work from an existing sense of abundance? | 1 | 2 | 3 | 4 | 5 |
| Do I lead my life and conduct my work in an original way, from a feeling of joy and cheerfulness? | 1 | 2 | 3 | 4 | 5 |
| Do I take breaks as needed to revive my inspiration? | 1 | 2 | 3 | 4 | 5 |
| Am I able to be gently assertive in a soulful way? | 1 | 2 | 3 | 4 | 5 |
| Can I speak the truth fearlessly and express myself authentically? | 1 | 2 | 3 | 4 | 5 |

| | ALWAYS | FREQUENTLY | SOMETIMES | INFREQUENTLY | NEVER |
|---|---|---|---|---|---|
| Do I respect other peoples' boundaries? | 1 | 2 | 3 | 4 | 5 |
| Does my presence inspire gratitude and love? | 1 | 2 | 3 | 4 | 5 |
| Do I silently emanate a feeling of love and oneness, particularly toward those who look up to me in some way? | 1 | 2 | 3 | 4 | 5 |
| Do I give credit to others where due? | 1 | 2 | 3 | 4 | 5 |
| Do I share my knowledge, money, and gifts with others as and when appropriate? | 1 | 2 | 3 | 4 | 5 |

*If you scored between 14 and 30 points, you are a role model, leader, and guide whom others can look up to and depend upon.*

*If you scored between 31 and 50 points, you will benefit from setting intentions to strengthen your integrity and, subsequently, your leadership.*

*If you scored between 51 and 70 points, it is time to embrace the confidence that developing greater integrity and alignment in terms of your values, speech, and actions will give you.*

# Leading with Integrity

*Fix an ideal-based intention for action, for the welfare of as many beings as possible.*

Having an ideal to motivate your actions empowers you to consistently make selfless decisions and to achieve greater heights in your work. The wider the circle of your ideal (to benefit not only your family but also your community, country, humanity, or ideally, all living beings), the more powerful it will be.

Contrast this with being driven by unselfish desires. Unselfish actions have benevolent underlying desires such as "I want a hundred thousand people to benefit from my work." In this case, you have a noble desire. But if the desire itself is connected to ego and you reach only fifty thousand people, for example, you may feel negative emotions like anger, sadness, disappointment, frustration, and lack of self-worth. Then you may stop performing the actions you were doing and will stop benefiting others. Your work becomes about you and your small ego.

The difference between a sage and an ordinary person lies in their reaction to the outcomes of their actions. A sage will act ceaselessly and tirelessly, performing the same actions as an ordinary person but with no attachment to what comes of them. A sage does not need to impact a certain number of people to feel contentment or worthiness, even if they have an ideal to serve as many beings as possible. We can learn from this by maintaining an unconditional commitment to a timeless ideal (versus time-bound incentives) so that we remain in the present moment (where our greatest power lies) versus visiting the past or future. It also gives you the power of consistency, which is required for success. Just as water moving in a single direction gains power, your actions gain power when they are consistently directed toward an elevated ideal.

### Honestly assess your personal gifts and propensities.

In the Vedic spiritual tradition, there are four main propensities that people fall into, according to their natural inclinations. Each is connected with one of the four goals of life. Those who seek to know the spiritual Self are spiritualists; they are most interested in pursuing the goal of spiritual liberation. Those who seek to protect higher values are spiritual warriors, who are most interested in the life goal of purpose (living by noble values). Those who seek wealth are most inclined to the life goal of abundance. And those who seek enjoyment are those most inclined toward the life goal of pleasure.

My primary propensity is that of a spiritualist. I also have an interest in protecting higher values as a spiritual warrior. I have always written, first in personal journals, then blogs, for publications, books, etc. Public speaking and teaching are things I have always done, and I have loved learning how to help people heal themselves by applying problem-solving skills to co-create comprehensive wellness plans for wellness seekers. I also love practicing and sharing Yoga and spiritual practices.

### Use your intellect to develop a plan for employing your gifts in service.

Your intellect is what empowers you to think, strategize, and plan. It is active, as opposed to the mind, which passively follows in the footsteps of predecessors and ancestors without questioning their behaviors. Swami Parthasarathy characterizes those who apply their intellect as "aggressive" and those who do not as "passive." He further distinguishes between those who are aggressively or passively good or aggressively or passively bad. Those who are passively good or bad passively do what those before them have done, for better or for worse. Those who are aggressively bad mercilessly scheme how they can manipulate people.

Goddess Siddhidhatri, who is beloved by all sages, gods, and yogis, gives us the power of intention, so that we may develop what Swami Parthasarathy calls "aggressive goodness." Lord Krishna is a perfect embodiment of aggressive goodness. He applied his intellect to foresee consequences, plan ahead, and effectively guide Arjuna the spiritual warrior to defeat the evil ways of his aggressively bad cousins on the opposing side of the battlefield in the Bhagavad Gita. Most of the time, aggressive goodness does not mean directly approaching someone and telling them they are corrupt.

As I wrote this book and applied my entrepreneurial skills to create a safe platform for authentic teaching of Vedic and other aligned ancient forms of spiritual wisdom, I wove into both projects the value of applied knowledge above theory alone. As E. F. Schumacher once wisely said, "An ounce of practice is generally worth more than a ton of theory." I built this approach to teaching into every aspect of my organization, including planning to only certify Ayurveda wellness practitioners who really live the teachings, to ensure there is integrity between what leaders I train say and what they do themselves. I truly believe that those who follow us (including children, if we are parents) follow only what we ourselves actually *do*, not what we say.

### Work with instrument consciousness, by doing what you discern you ought to do.

Service, in whatever capacity you offer it, whether as a parent, teacher, organizational leader, or a sports team captain, means to help others who seek support. It also means inspiring courage in others to grow toward self-sufficiency. Service, in this sense, is an act of godliness, and the intention to serve is one that emerges within those of us who experience our true Self (divinity) unfolding.

Instrument consciousness means being an instrument for the divine to flow through. It involves deeply acknowledging that all the talents we possess are gifts from the divine and, therefore, behaving without vanity or the belief that we alone are responsible for our achievements. Instrument consciousness recognizes the presence of all the visible and invisible beings that have contributed to any positive ability or blessing in our lives. It also means acting in a way wherein we are true to ourselves and our own intentions.

When I act with instrument consciousness in my work as the leader of an organization, I feel as though I am not "doing" anything at all. I don't teach any differently, whether I am sharing with a hundred people or just one person. It is all the same to me, because the most important thing is simply to flow in service of my higher intentions.

Acting with instrument consciousness empowers me to discern feedback I receive from students and others so that I can ascertain whether feedback comes from an intention to further their ability to practice the teachings or simply from a desire to consume information for information's sake (a desire that obstructs spiritual progress). It is a teacher's responsibility to answer questions from students, which I always do, even if it means repeating myself by answering similar questions time and again. I do so patiently because I understand that reinforcement and repetition are necessary for the learning process. I feel tremendous contentment and satisfaction in doing merely what I ought to do without being attached to any particular outcome.

I see my organization as a healing garden that we all can visit freely to remember our spiritual power. Sometimes, as a gardener teacher, I have to cut away "weeds" of ignorance in students that cause them to hurt themselves. Other times, I must simply water the flowers, so to speak, and ensure they receive enough sunlight. Then, in Goddess Siddhidhatri's divine timing, I often experience the pure pleasure of seeing my students blossom with radiant health and spiritual empowerment. Approaching my organizational leadership as being like tending to a garden helps ensure that I constantly discern what I also ought to do to keep my own body and mind pure and flowing so that I can sustain showing up unconditionally and keep flowing like a river, without stress, worry, fears, or complaints.

### Bring a spirit of humility, authenticity, and transparency into your leadership.

Humility is the insignia of one who bears great knowledge per the Vedic spiritual tradition. The more knowledge you have, the more you realize how much you do not know, and the humbler you become. Humility also means recognizing that we all have a part to play in the grand scheme of our work and our lives. Everyone has different talents, and just because one person is a "leader" does not mean this person is superior to anyone else on the team.

Authenticity and transparency empower us to serve in a way that inspires those we lead to know and trust us, which makes for stronger relationships that can give way to the kind of cooperation and teamwork that is required to achieve anything meaningful in life.

I make it a point for my own organization to be a safe place for people to be as vulnerable as they need to be for their own growth. I know that it is my role to have the courage to share openly and honestly and to help others feel safe enough to do the same within the group and with each other when I pair them as community buddies. I recognize that my sacred duty as a teacher is to lead by example, to demonstrate, first and foremost, what it means to love my true Self. I am clear that I want to give back from a space of gratitude for all the blessings I have received in my life, because sharing these blessings is what I ought to do.

### Lead in a way that keeps you free from dependency and sets those you lead free as well.

Sovereignty (especially emotional sovereignty) is the ultimate goal of human birth. It is the highest value any human being can strive to achieve. It is what makes self-actualization (fulfillment of your talents) possible on a worldly level and what makes Self-realization (knowing who you are at the deepest core, in every situation) possible on a spiritual level.

I stayed in complete solitude for a full year and a half during the COVID-19 pandemic, without seeing any of my family members and connecting in person with friends only a handful of times, and navigating the comings and goings of three intense romantic relationships during the pandemic was an incredibly empowering experience for me. Because abandonment is a core wound of mine from childhood, this experience showed me that I truly am emotionally independent and strong enough within my love for my own Self to withstand when people once close to me are no longer part of my life. In the extended time I spent alone, I discovered that I am content within myself and not dependent on anything but knowing my true Self to experience love and joy.

As a leader, I practice doing what I ought to do physically, by preparing material for classes and showing up each time to teach, answering questions and sharing follow-up information. Emotionally, I truly love my students, just as I love everyone in my life (even those who have hurt me). Intellectually, I intend to always have a charitable disposition toward my students, meaning I ensure that whatever I give them is offered to the divinity within them and encourages their self-reliance versus dependency upon me.

I can see how my own personal spiritual practice has become the foundation for sharing what I have been blessed to learn and experience with others. And in setting my intention in service of health and spiritual empowerment for all, I return myself to the power of practice (the theme of chapter 1 and the first chakra) to concretize and ground my selfless intention into living reality. The Navratri spiritual practice, in this way, is an endless, cyclical journey where one step leads to potentially infinite steps, all leading us back home, to our own true Self.

# The Path Forward: Practices for Intentionality

PRACTICE: *Define an intention for living by noble values.*

One of the four goals of human life is to live by noble values, which is one of the many definitions of the word *dharma*. According to one of the ancient Vedic sages, dharma includes ten specific noble values: truthfulness, patience, forgiveness, mental strength, non-stealing, cleanliness, self-control, wisdom, seeking knowledge, and not reacting in anger.

When you define an intention for living by a noble value that resonates deeply within your being, it gives you an anchor for your spiritual journey, to cultivate the power of Goddess Siddhidhatri in your life. Cultivating any one of these values is also a complete spiritual journey in itself, which can help you progress tremendously by narrowing your focus to one value that causes you to automatically cultivate other related noble values.

For example, if you wish to practice self-control, then you will automatically employ greater patience, practice forgiveness, and not react in anger.

PRACTICE: *Create a personal vision statement to incorporate a new virtue into your life.*

It is such a powerful practice to reflect upon a specific way you envision bringing a new virtue into your daily life as a way to create a safe container for yourself to begin. For example, if you wish to develop more courage, it first makes a big difference to define what courage looks and feels like for you. How will you look when you're being courageous? What will your body feel like? What would developing more courage empower you to do that you are not currently able to do?

Write a vision for what manifesting more courage in your life would take for you. Are there specific situations right now that make you feel afraid? Can you imagine the particular circumstances that make it hardest for you to be courageous right now? Write down baby steps for what it will feel like to start practicing courage in those challenging situations.

For example, I struggled with whether to actively participate in or remain quiet during group meetings for almost a whole year after transitioning into a new role at THE WELL. But eventually I saw that progressing in terms of expressing myself when I had something to share meant setting a minimal goal of contributing at least once per meeting. Once I set this minimum standard, I felt much more alive and engaged in meetings, and I was able to offer suggestions and guidance on different initiatives. After a couple of meetings, I started to feel more comfortable speaking up and expressing myself in my role. The confidence I gained from doing this empowered me to start speaking up for myself in other situations afterward.

Each step you make toward manifesting your virtue helps you to embody it more and more naturally, so that it becomes a core part of who you are and part of your overall character. You can ask Goddess Siddhidhatri within you to guide you to create as clear of a vision statement as possible and to support you with manifesting new virtues in your life.

PRACTICE: *Create a personal mantra to put the power of a wellness practice into action.*

The power of intention begins with your personal "why" for putting a wellness practice into action. Creating your own personalized mantra for practice is a beautiful way to connect with your intention on a regular basis. Some examples of personal mantras you can draw inspiration from in creating your own include:

- My body is my temple.
- "Service is the rent we pay for the privilege of living on earth." –Shirley Chisholm
- "Life shrinks or expands in proportion to your courage." –Anaïs Nin

My personal mantra for participation and showing up fully to my role is simply to "do what I ought to do." In Sanskrit, the famous word *karma* has more meanings than "what goes around comes around." It also means "action." There are three kinds of actions we can perform:

1. Selfish actions, full of desires to benefit only ourselves

2. Unselfish actions, full of desires to benefit others

   Both of these actions generate more karma (in the sense of consequences that mirror our actions). The karma that returns may be positive or negative. To move your spiritual journey forward in an evolutionary way that does not cause you to create any more karma requires performing a third type of action, which is defined as pure action.

3. Selfless or pure actions, without any kind of desire, simply doing what you ought to do

   For example, if you are a teacher, then you ought to teach. If you are a singer, then you ought to sing. If you are a painter, then you ought to paint. The more pure our actions, the more motivated we are by our "why," the more free we feel, and the more we evolve spiritually. This is the way that Goddess Siddhidhatri can lead us to the ultimate goal of human life, which is spiritual liberation.

**PRACTICE: *Create an intention to achieve prosperity that also involves giving back.***

Achieving prosperity is another of the four goals of human life in ancient wisdom traditions. We can only sustain giving back from the foundation of having material stability in our lives. And ancient wisdom traditions reveal how the more you give, the more comes to you, as a conduit of abundance.

Donating to good causes that uplift other beings is a beautiful way to connect with the abundant nature of Goddess Siddhidhatri within you. Set an intention to contribute a portion of what you make so that you bring a more selfless spirit of service into your work. The more selfless your intention for achieving prosperity, the more your work can help lead you to spiritual liberation (the ultimate quest of life and the spiritual journey of Navratri).

This is because work is an area of our lives where we can otherwise get lost in desires for more—more fame, recognition, status, power, etc. Being clear on your intention for work to be a pure vessel for uplifting as many people as possible through the prosperity you achieve empowers you to work toward a higher ideal of service that helps prevent you from getting caught in desire-ridden traps. It also helps transform your work into a spiritual practice in which you can focus on the three keys to success in all your actions: concentration (being fully present in the moment), consistency, and cooperation (cultivating a team spirit). This is all the power of Goddess Siddhidhatri in your ninth chakra in practice.

PRACTICE: *Craft a strategy to experience pleasure without getting lost in or addicted to it.*

Experiencing pleasure is another of the four goals of human life in the ancient Vedic spiritual tradition. There is nothing wrong with pleasure in and of itself. It's simply when you want more and more of it that it becomes a trap of endless desire.

One of the signs you are progressing on your spiritual journey is the length of time and intensity of your emotional reactions to situations that upset you. Another sign of spiritual growth is not craving more pleasure when it comes your way.

This is something you can cultivate by creating a personal strategy for yourself in terms of how you can embrace the pleasures of life within healthy limits. The best limits are those you set for yourself, based on a personal conviction of the "why" behind your personal limits. This process of creating well-defined boundaries around your pleasure, with the support of Goddess Siddhidhatri, is a way to take ownership for your enjoyment. This ensures that you can enjoy your chocolate cake versus your chocolate cake enjoying you (as happens in cases of addiction!).

So if you love chocolate cake, for example, then can you figure out a way to still be able to enjoy it but not suffer as a result of consuming it? Perhaps that means limiting it to a once-a-month treat. Or if you are really having trouble weaning yourself off it, then can you figure out a way to reduce your daily or weekly consumption of it to an amount that won't harm you? The more you can practice letting go of your desire for chocolate cake, the more you will actually be able to enjoy it when you do so in moderation.

## PRACTICE: *Write an intention to further your spiritual growth.*

Your spiritual journey is one that you ultimately choose, all on your own. We are born alone, and we shall die alone. In between our birth and death, we have a relatively short window of time in which to progress and evolve spiritually. Your progress upon your spiritual path is totally up to you. Writing your intention amplifies it and makes it much more concrete.

Every year, for a special ancient celebration of the guru (which actually means "the remover of darkness") on a full moon day in July, I've written an intention in order to advance my spiritual growth. I usually place it somewhere I can see it often, to remind myself of the intention and to guide my ego through the painful emotional experiences that come with being human. For a whole year, in 2016, I focused my journey around letting go of shame, and it significantly lessened the amount of shame I experienced on a regular basis.

One year, it was all about reclaiming the power of my soul, no matter what. That led to a series of profound life changes, culminating in moving cross-country, to restart my life on my own terms. During another year, I set an intention to experience the power of the goddess within me to win a victory over all obstacles, inner as well as outer. That was an incredible year of conquering many inner demons, including those that surfaced in writing this book.

Allow yourself some time each ninth day of your practice to receive your intention for your spiritual growth from your higher Self. It's okay if it doesn't come to you right away. Simply making space will lead you naturally toward it. And when you eventually set your intention, know that it shall set into motion the exact circumstances in your life that will empower you to realize it. When you do achieve victories on your spiritual journey, make sure to bow to Siddhidhatri within you. There are divine forces always present to guide us, if only we tune in to hear their inner guidance for us.

## PRACTICE: *Find a way to give back to nature daily.*

Mother Earth is a goddess whom we must give back to, out of gratitude for the bounty that nature provides us to take care of all our needs, each and every day. We can connect more deeply to our higher Self by making it a daily priority to give back to the one who gifts us everything.

Setting an intention to give back to nature may look like stepping up your recycling game as an offering to Goddess Siddhidhatri within you. It may involve researching local nature conservation efforts and seeing how you can contribute—your time, money, or skills—to supporting them. It may mean switching to all-natural cleaning products and personal hygiene products that are not tested on animals and good for the environment. You could volunteer your time at a local animal shelter or choose to offer a foster home to animals from these shelters.

As you give back to nature, you will likely find that your appreciation of the many gifts of nature expands each day, blessing you with greater optimism, strength, and mental clarity to go through the ups and downs of life.

**PRACTICE:** *Give to a person or group of people who are in need.*

There is a transformative quality when you render service to those in need without any attachments or expectations. It is particularly important to discern that those you are considering serving have no other way to receive what you have to give them. And that you can give with a spirit of not identifying as the giver–but rather serving as an instrument for blessings to reach worthy recipients who are currently without what you have to offer.

It also helps to consider how you can support others to become more independent in some way in their own lives. Rather than simply giving money to the poor, are there ways you can support local or international organizations that support the poor to learn skills that will allow them to better their own lives? Can you donate some of your own time and skills that come naturally to you to such organizations? Doing so is activating the power of Siddhidhatri within your ninth chakra, so that this giving becomes part of your regular spiritual practice, through which you can really practice discernment and detachment from your identification with your actions. In that way, you become a pure vessel for the gifts (financial, material, or talents) you have received.

**PRACTICE:** *Share a skill or teach others something you know.*

In the ancient wisdom traditions, the best teachers are those who are *renunciates,* or basically those who do not in any way wish to hoard or prevent others from learning and knowing what they themselves know. When you can pass along what you have been blessed to learn in your life, particularly any spiritual lessons, you are able to complete a beautiful cycle of giving back from a place of inner fullness.

It doesn't matter how many lives you reach or what your impact is in a quantitative sense. It just matters that, if you are able to do something that others are not, you can share, as a way to simply do what you ought to do, for the greatest good of all. This is one of the highest expressions of the power of Siddhidhatri within you.

## Conclusion

# Celebrating the Victory of Light over Darkness

ON THE TENTH DAY OF EACH NAVRATRI CYCLE, I ACKNOWLEDGE THE journey of the previous nine days and the internal (and subsequently external) transformations each one unfailingly leads to.

Today, at the conclusion of writing this book, I feel simultaneously powerful beyond anything I could have ever imagined and also vulnerable and humbled at the divine force that orchestrates all events of our lives for the unfolding of our true Self, if only we surrender to follow the guidance that comes from deep within.

Having matured by consistently pushing myself to live by the spiritual teachings I learned from the Vedic tradition over the course of more than a decade, I feel extremely grateful for the role these teachings played in empowering me to save myself. In the face of different kinds of darkness and difficulties that unfolded over the years of my spiritual journey, it was the teachings, and my commitment to applying them with devotion in my heart, that protected me in the end. I knew I had truly found Goddess Durga in myself when I navigated an extremely devastating experience of boundary violations, harassment, scapegoating, and betrayal with clarity, discernment, and detachment. Because I truly understood the law of karma, I was able to take radical responsibility for all the difficulties in my life, see their interconnectedness, and maintain my equanimity throughout the situations that tested my spiritual growth. I stayed centered in my true Self through it all and transcended that time in order to restart my life and live out the purpose I was meant to fulfill.

I feel very grateful to my parents for how fully and unconditionally they showed up for me during this dark period of my life. When I see them today, I cannot help but feel immense gratitude for the entire journey of the past decade, which had a difficult beginning but is now brimming with peace, true harmony, and love. By remaining steadfast in my spiritual practices and strengthening my relationship with my true Self, I was able to heal my deepest wounds and transform my relationship with my parents and all others I had difficulties with. All healing truly begins by resolving to win the war within, first and foremost.

The male deities entrust Goddess Durga to battle and overcome the greatest demon, whom none of the male deities could defeat themselves. No matter how dark another person's behaviors may be, the greatest demon is actually in our own minds. Once we have overcome our own anger, fear, resistance, laziness, self-doubt, and self-destructive tendencies, we realize that there is, in fact, no outer demon. There is no dark force "out there" that can destroy us. It is we who are our greatest benefactor, and we who can become our own greatest downfall.

Many of my family members and others close to me have told me over the years that my goodness, kindness, compassion, and naivete were weaknesses that made me vulnerable to outer evil. In fact, I feel that it was my very goodness, compassion, and kindness that were my saving graces, that supported me in winning the war within when I finally vowed to be as kind to myself as I would ever be to anyone else–no matter what. I own my reality, and I exercise the power of my intellect by constantly questioning everything. I don't take anything for granted. My self-love, spiritual practices, and ability to discern what is true and detach from all that is not divine, within and without, are my greatest strengths. With the power of years of devoted spiritual practice behind me, I have surrendered myself to Goddess Durga within me. I became my own hero, savior, and protector.

Today, I lead my own organization to carry forward the spiritual lineage traditions of Baba Ayodhya Nath Sinha, who learned and received it from his father, Bade Baba Shanti Prakash, and that of my personal Ayurveda ancestors, Amarchand Khokhani, Hakemchand Khokhani, Surchand Khokhani, and all those who came before them. Not a single day goes by when I do not feel grateful for all the experiences I survived, and for the opportunity to share all the gems I gained from the Navratri journey. I can honestly say that it was all worth it, to dive to the bottom of the ocean of my own emotional suffering to retrieve the precious pearl of my true Self.

I wrote this book because I felt it was what I ought to do, in service of the victory of the eternal light of the highest Truth, which ultimately sets us all free.

May you, in reading this honest account of my experiences, find within yourself the strength, power, and light to dispel any darkness you may presently be suffering from and, in the process, become your own hero.

There is a saying in the ancient Vedic spiritual tradition, which goes *Om Tat Sat.* It means that darkness is temporary, and the light of the

Ultimate Truth is all there is. May we all bow, over and over again, to that light, which symbolically resides in the center of the garba dance, representing the power we all have to give birth to our true Self, which connects us with all living beings in an endless, beautiful circular dance of life.

## OM TAT SAT

# Acknowledgments

I AM DEEPLY GRATEFUL TO THE MANY PEOPLE WITHOUT WHOM THIS book could have never been birthed:

First, I thank Vijaya Jhothi, whose very name means "the victory of the light of the Truth," for inspiring me to discover my true Self.

I thank my literary agent, Lisa DiMona, for believing in this book from day one, and supporting me each step of the way to write it.

I, quite literally, could not have written this challenging book without the constant guidance, support, and collaboration of Julie Mosow, who has been an incredible ally in my quest to be true to myself, all the way.

Deep gratitude to Gautam Mulchandani, Uncle Mitch Hall, Rita Ellen Mirchandani, Shweta Bhatt, and Tanvi Jain for serving as astute beta readers and providing me endless love and support.

Huge thanks to Marian Lizzi at TarcherPerigee for her astute feedback and support, and to her entire team for making this book come to life: copyeditor Madeline Hopkins, production editor Andrea St. Aubin, cover designer Caroline Johnson, and interior designer Shannon Plunkett.

Thanks to Lia Love Avellino for sharing her insightful letter-writing practices of behavioral change and emotional regulation and transformation.

I am forever grateful to Mukta Maria de Blum, Silvana Fillmore, and Betty Payne for being my three angel goddesses who each walked with me and supported me as I spread my wings to fly.

I am deeply grateful to Baiju Mohandas for teaching me the art of Kalaripayattu, so I can always feel confident and safe in my own skin and feel prepared to meet any future "worst-case scenarios" with an assurance I have never known before.

Eternal thanks to my parents and sister for all the ways they have challenged me to grow and then supported me in following the pathless path of my soul.

# Appendix

THE GAYATRI MANTRA IS THE GREATEST GIFT I RECEIVED FROM MY SPIRitual studies. It is a prayer to evoke the light of the true Self within us all, which the outer sun is a reflection and reminder of in nature.

It goes like this:

*Om Bhur Bhuvah Svaha*

*Tat Savitur Varenyam*

*Bhargo Devasya Dhimahi*

*Dhiyo Yonah Prachodayat*

You can visit my organization's website, theancientway.co, to listen to a recording of it.

# Resources

warrior and discover your true Self.

## *True to Yourself* Podcast

@ananta.one on iTunes, Spotify, Google Podcasts, iHeartRadio and other channels

Listen to the *True to Yourself* podcast for a compassionate guide to coming home to your true Self.

## Spiritual Warrior Certification Program

theancientway.co/spiritualwarrior

Become your own hero in the company of other heroes as part of the Spiritual Warrior Certification Program to prepare to lead a life of integrity and give back as a teacher, parent, author, or entrepreneur by following each step of the Navratri practice for internal transformation. This program has an optional Counseling Training and Launch Accelerator to support you with practical business skills and book development to manifest your visions into the world.

## Circle of Life Community Program

theancientway.co/community

Join a community wellness movement that will connect you with fellow spiritual wellness seekers around the world for power of practice circles, application-oriented spiritual teachings, delicious seasonal Ayurvedic recipes, embodiment classes, and healing sessions.

## The Ancient Way

theancientway.co

Visit my organization's website to learn how you can benefit from our online and in-person courses, retreats, and community programs. You can also check out lots of delicious Ayurvedic food for your soul here.

## *The Ayurveda Way*

Read my first book, *The Ayurveda Way*, to learn 108 simple, doable wellness practices from the world's oldest healing system for better sleep, less stress, optimal digestion, and more.

## Vedanta World E-Learning Program

elearning.vedantaworld.org

Learn the art of living by studying the spiritual science of Vedanta systematically online with recordings of the renowned philosopher saint Swami Parthasarathy's lectures on the Bhagavad Gita, Upanishads, and many other important Vedic spiritual texts, verse by verse.

## THE WELL

the-well.com

Visit THE WELL to experience integrated offerings that deliver personalized, holistic health care via programs and spaces that bring together the best of Eastern and Western healing modalities.

# About the Author

ANANTA RIPA AJMERA is a spiritual teacher and cofounder and CEO of The Ancient Way, an organization that serves as a bridge between ancient wisdom and modern living that supports you to embody wisdom in a way that unfolds your true Self. She is the host of the *True to Yourself* podcast, advisor of Ayurveda at THE WELL (a modern integrative wellness space), and author of the award-winning book *The Ayurveda Way*.

Ananta has taught Ayurveda at Stanford Medicine, New York University, UNICEF,

Photograph of the author by Joe Orecchio

ABC News, and the California Department of Public Health, and her work has been featured in *Vogue*, *Forbes*, and *Yoga Journal* and on Fox News. She presently leads a Spiritual Warrior Certificate Program, Circle of Life Community Program, and an Ayurveda practitioner program. Visit theancientway.co for more. You can also follow Ananta on Instagram and Facebook @ananta.one.